Shadow Work

Comprehensive
Workbook & Journal
for Inner Understanding & Healing

Table of Content

Chapter III - Emotions are Navigating Our Life

Judgment
Fear and Avoidance
Hurt and Pain
Jealousy and Envy
Guilt and Regret
Shame
Anxiety

Chapter IV - The Inner Child Lives Forever

What is unresolved (holding on)
Generational wounding
What have my parents taught me?
The values of my family
What was praised in my family?
What was forbidden in my family?

Chapter V - Wishes and Dreams

Expectations
If I could have been anything...
How do I envision my future?
Memorable Dreams

Chapter VI - Healing Open Wounds

Grounding
Breath
Gratitude
Love
Trust
Inspiration
Creativity

Ending Words from a Therapist

Introduction
The Concept of The Shadow

Hey there, curious minds and introspective explorers! Today, we're embarking on an exhilarating journey through the enchanting realms of ego self-identification and, as a result, the shadow aspect of our self. Buckle up, because we're about to dive into the fascinating world where "me," "myself," and "I" dance in a dazzling waltz of identity.

Rooted in the depths of our unconscious mind, the concept of the shadow has fascinated and mystified thinkers, psychologists, and seekers of self-awareness for centuries. This enigmatic aspect of our psyche was first introduced by Swiss psychiatrist Carl Jung. His theory has given rise to a transformative practice known as shadow work. In this introduction, we explore the origins of the shadow concept, the dimensions it encompasses, and the profound activities that constitute shadow work.

As Jung delved deep into the human psyche, he unearthed a reservoir of unacknowledged and repressed aspects that he termed the "shadow." In his groundbreaking theories, the shadow represented the repository of all that we deny, disown, or find unacceptable within ourselves. These aspects include our fears, insecurities, desires, and untamed emotions, often pushed into the subconscious due to societal norms, upbringing, and personal experiences.

Jung believed that the shadow, if left unexplored, could profoundly influence our lives, manifesting in unconscious behaviors, patterns, and projections onto others.

By acknowledging and integrating these hidden facets, individuals could unlock profound growth, healing, and self-awareness. The shadow concept, thus, was born as a doorway to a deeper understanding of one's authentic self.

Shadow work is a therapeutic and introspective practice aimed at bringing the shadow self into conscious awareness. As the saying goes, "What we resist persists." Shadow work encapsulates the recognition that confronting and embracing our darkness will pave the way for profound transformation and personal empowerment.

This transformative process encompasses various psychological, emotional, and spiritual dimensions. It involves navigating through the labyrinth of suppressed emotions, childhood wounds, and societal conditioning. Shadow work is not about dwelling on negativity but about transmuting it into self-awareness and wholeness.

A shadow work workbook serves as a compass, offering structured exercises and prompts that facilitate the journey into the depths of one's psyche. These activities are carefully curated to foster self-discovery, healing, and transformation. Some key activities in the shadow work include journaling, guided meditations and visualizations, awareness, creative expression, and rituals.

Made by a psychotherapist, the Shadow Work Journal for Inner Understanding and Healing can be your guide to living a conscious, fulfilling life. We use this opportunity to salute your inner strength and bravery for diving into your personality's dark, unconscious parts.

A Few Words From The Therapist

Shadow Work in extensive self-awareness, self-knowledge, and self-understanding process. During your work, you will discover a lot of unpleasant thoughts, emotions, personal experiences, tendencies, or simply patterns of behavior. And, naturally, they will be hard to process.

This is why I warmly recommend that you take your time with this workbook. The point is not to finish it quickly but to gain the most you can out of it. There is a psychological process known as "incubation." It represents the seemingly "empty" times when you don't overwhelm yourself and overthink but instead do go around your day, crossing tasks off of your list, buying groceries, commuting to work, or hanging around with your partner. It is during this time that awareness and unconscious processing of new experiences happens. Giving yourself time to "incubate" the awareness can help you understand yourself better and implement the changes you want in your life.

For the outcome, I recommend you do one section at a time. A few different exercises and writing prompts are part of one section, and they all hold the same title for your convenience.

I also recommend that you open and work with this book when you have time, energy, privacy, and emotional willingness. Will will ensure that your whole Self and system is included, present, and engaged.

Last but not least, I also recommend that you keep this workbook somewhere private.

You will uncover and write about a lot of possibly uncomfortable topics. My biggest concern is not about feelings of embarrassment or shame if someone reads it thought. My concern is about having and maintaining social boundaries, respecting your needs, and protecting your privacy.

In the end, I would like to finish my speech with words of appreciation and support. I salute your willingness to work on yourself, become the best version possible, and improve your inner well-being, emotional state, mindset, relationships, and overall life. Shadow work requires strength, honesty, dedication, and persistence. And by taking this workbook, you show all those things.

The road can be quite bumpy, so make sure that you show yourself a lot of self-love, self-appreciation, understanding, and support. In the end, no mental work and improvement will matter if it isn't done with a lot of self-love. Things change only after we fully accept and embrace them as they are.

Wishing you fruitful work,

Author and Therapist

Letter of
Dedication and Determination

I,_____

will focus myself and my efforts to

work through this journal and

workbook with

dedication and determination.

Date of start _____

Date of finish _____

Signature

Chapter I
Ego and The Shadow

Picture this: you're standing in front of a mirror, and you can't help but strike a pose – your signature smirk, the perfect hair flip, and an imaginary acceptance speech for that Nobel Prize you're yet to win. Well, welcome to the grand show put on by your ego, the star of the self-identification spectacle!

But what exactly is this ego thing? Imagine it as your personal stage director, the master of ceremonies of your self-concept. The voice that says, "Hey, that's my favorite color!" or "I'm not a morning person; please don't talk to me until I've had my third cup of coffee." In a world where individuality is the name of the game, the ego is the backbone that holds the self together.

Let's take it from the start. The concept of the Ego was first introduced by the grand (or, if you ask others, the not-so-grand) neurologist Sigmund Freud, the founder of psychoanalysis.

The Ego was part of Freud's Holy Trinity - the Id, the Ego, and the Superego. The Id is instinctual and impulsive - it only wants what it wants. Name it - the animal in us. The Superego is our moral compass, or the saint, if you will. The Ego is the part torn between these two - it's the aspect that mediates communication and tries to fulfill the needs of the remaining two aspects. To make it as simple as it gets - The Id wants food, and it wants it now. The Superego says, "Yea, well, you can't steal." And the Ego is here to mediate and decide whether to ask for a bite or simply go buy something.

Now, these are the basics. Psychology and psychotherapy have since moved further down the road. Today, under the concept of the Ego, we include the things we identify with and believe to be.

Let's bring the conversation closer to how Jung explained the ego. After all, the concepts of the Shadow are his, so it would only be fair to determine the ego from the same viewpoint. Basically, Jung explains the ego as the center of consciousness, containing our awarenesses. The ego organizes our experiences, memories, emotions, and thoughts, making our life a continuum of personal identity.

Now, once we better understand the ego, we can more easily dive into the concept of the Shadow. The Shadow is everything that our Ego doesn't want to identify with. To put it into his own words -"The shadow personifies everything that the subject refuses to acknowledge about himself."

In this sense, the Shadow becomes the polarity of our Ego, the black to our white, the dark in our light. And, the truth is - we have them both. But, since the point of the Ego is to keep our personality in check, the idea of a Shadow, or having an opposite, becomes an unbearing thought. So, the ego often "fights" to avoid facing the shadow. That is, to acknowledge that everything it doesn't identify with - still exists within the Self.

This chapter will start the process of becoming aware of the Shadow by acknowledging our ego's polarity.

My Intelectual Representation
of Ego and Shadow

Write down how you understand the concepts of the Ego and the Shadow. Write words that come to mind, associations, fantasies, or previous experiences.

_____

_____

_____

_____

_____

_____

_____

_____

_____

_____

_____

_____

_____

_____

_____

_____

_____

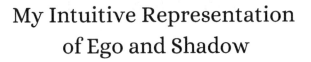

My Intuitive Representation
of Ego and Shadow

Now, close your eyes and try to visualize what the Ego and the Shadow would look like if they had a physical form.

Focus on determining their shape, material, color, substance, or any other attribute you might give to them.

Draw and paint the visual representations.

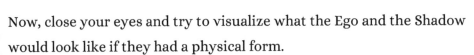

Words of Wisdom

The ultimate aim of the ego is not to see something, but to be something.

Muhammad Iqbal

The development and size of the shadow runs parallel to that of the ego and its defenses.

Jolande Jacobi

Your ego can become an obstacle to your work. If you start believing in your greatness, it is the death of your creativity.

Marina Abramovic

All you need to know and observe in yourself is this: Whenever you feel superior or inferior to anyone, that's the ego in you.

Eckhart Tolle

A bad day for your ego is a great day for your soul.

Jillian Michaels

Ego Self

When we dive into Shadow work, we ought to start with what is familiar to us. Our Ego, that is.
From the awareness of what we identify with, we can start lookng at the things we push away into the Shadow.

My Physical Body - Exercise

Stand in front of a mirror. Silently look at yourself and your physical features.
After some time, start gazing at your own eyes in the mirror. Maintain self-eye-contact as long as you can.
When suitable, tell yourself something in the mirror. Say the first thing that comes to mind.

In the next step, just close your eyes and try to visualize yourself, in full detail. Make the visualization in the space in front of you, as if you're seeing yourself from the side.
Carefully and with detailing start with the top of your head (hair) and move your way through your face. Dedicate time to each feature, mentally describing it as you place it in the visualization.
After each added feature, stop for a second to evaluate the mental description your gave.

Do you like this mental description? If not, how can you reframe it to be more positive?

Work your way though your whole body, finishing up with your toes.

Lastly, switch your visualization into your body. You're not seeing yourself from the side anymore, you're feeling yourself from inside. Go over each physical feature and tell yourself the reframed description.

What do I identify with?
Journaling

Introduce yourself. Write everything that comes to mind, as if you are introducing yourself to somebody else.
Write about what you do, who you are as a person, what you want to do and everything else that comes to mind.

_____

_____
_____
_____
_____
_____
_____
_____
_____
_____
_____
_____
_____
_____
_____
_____
_____
_____
_____
_____
_____
_____
_____

What do I identify with?
My Personality Traits

A big part of our Ego consciousness is based on the personality traits we identify with.

On the left, write down some of your personality traits. Choose the ones you most identify with. On the right, write down one situation where you have expressed named personality trait.

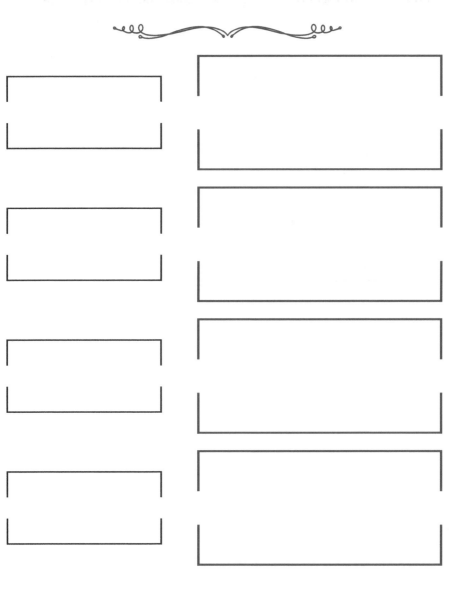

My Shadow Personality Traits

Once you've named key personality traits your Ego identifies with, it's time to provoke yourself by stating the polarities.

In the corresponding box on the left, write down the opposite personality trait of the one you named on the previous page.

For example, a polarity of "caring" could be "selfish", "egoistic", "apathetic" or something else. Once you write the polarities, write at least one situation where you expressed those personality traits.

What do I identify with?
My Roles

The roles we play in our life as a big part of what we identify with.

The term "roles" regards the socially acceptable behaviors we do, depending on the societal role we are playing.

For example, when we are at work, we play the "role" of an "employee", an "accountant", or a "manager." At home, we turn into the "roles" of a "daughter", a "spouse", a "father" or a "neighbor". Then, we also have different roles when we are friends, customers, acquaintances, or something else.

Below, there are some sentences with empty spaces. In the first sentence name a role that you are usually playing, and in the second sentence, explain the way in which you fulfill that role. Follow the example to have a clear picture of the instructions.

I'm a _____ _daughter._ _____. As such, I _always listen to my parents_ _and rarely disobey them. I go out of my way to help them and even if I'm_ _exhausted, I find time to visit or call._ _____ _I am a good, obedient daughter and my parents are proud of me._ _____ _____.

I'm a _____. As such, I _____ _____ _____ _____ _____.

What do I identify with?
My Roles

I'm a _____. As such, I _____
_____
_____
_____
_____.

I'm a _____. As such, I _____
_____
_____
_____
_____.

I'm a _____. As such, I _____
_____
_____
_____
_____.

I'm a _____. As such, I _____
_____
_____
_____
_____.

Now, ask yourself these questions about each role:
- Do I want this role? Am I happy with it?
- Is the behavior I do based on my standards, or societal ones?
- How can I improve this role to make it suit me better?
- What am I sacrificing to maintain this role as it "needs to be"?

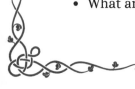

The Inner Critic

Deep within the recesses of the human mind, a persistent and often insidious voice resides—the inner critic.

The inner critic is that relentless inner monologue that scrutinizes, questions, and critiques our every move. Originating from a combination of societal influences, early upbringing, and personal experiences, this internalized voice assumes the role of a harsh evaluator, frequently focusing on perceived flaws, mistakes, and inadequacies.

Paradoxically, the inner critic emerges from a place of self-preservation, aiming to protect us from potential failures, unwanted emotions, and social rejection. It draws attention to areas that might need improvement, nudging us toward growth.

However, the inner critic's well-intentioned caution often spirals into a destructive force, sabotaging our self-esteem and stifling our potential. This duality underscores the complexity of the inner critic, a force that both propels and hinders our journey of self-discovery.

This is why it's essential to bring awareness to our Inner critic, the words and methods it uses to direct your behavior and the reasons behind the whole ordeal.

In the next parts, you can do all this and finish the process off by showing compassion and understanding for your Inner Critic. Yet again, you would also find ways to tame it and turn it from a degrading voice into an empowering one.

How does the Inner Critic talk?

First, you need to know how your Inner Critic talks with you. To increase awareness, answer the questions below.

Write 5 most common things you criticize yourself about. Write them in third person, singular, as if you're saying them to somebody else.
If able, elaborate on the criticism and try to use the exact words that you tend to tell to yourself.

_____

_____

_____

_____

_____

_____

_____

_____

_____

_____

_____

_____

_____

_____

_____

_____

_____

_____

_____

_____

Why does the Inner Critic talk like that?

Now, read one sentence at a time and answer these questions for each.

- Does this statement sound like someone else you know?
- Have you heard the criticism when you were young?
- If yes, who has said it to you?
- If no, what experience made your inner critic say this?
- Have you been repeating the criticized thing multiple times?
- If yes, why do you do that?
- If no, why does your Inner Critic keeps mentioning it?

Write your thoughts in the space below. You can write shortly about each criticizing message, or dedicate more space to the ones that really made you go "hmmm."

_____

_____

_____

_____

_____

_____

_____

_____

_____

_____

_____

_____

_____

_____

_____

Understanding the Inner Critic

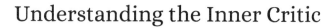

Use this exercise to dive into the reasons of the Inner Critic.

1.   Find a quiet and comfortable place to sit undisturbed for a few minutes.
2.   Close your eyes and take a few deep breaths to relax your mind and body.
3.   Imagine your inner critic as a separate persona or character. Give it a name if you'd like.
4.   Begin a written dialogue with your inner critic. Write a question or statement directed at your inner critic, and then allow it to respond in writing. For example, you could start with, "Why do you always criticize me?"
5.   As you engage in this dialogue, allow your inner critic to express its concerns, fears, and intentions. Write down its responses without judgment.
6.   Once your inner critic has shared its perspective, respond to it from a place of self-compassion and understanding. Write down counterarguments or alternative viewpoints that challenge the inner critic's negative statements.
7.   Continue this written dialogue for as long as you feel comfortable. Aim for a balanced conversation that acknowledges both the concerns of your inner critic and your own compassionate responses.

Conclude the dialogue by expressing gratitude to your inner critic for trying to protect you while also affirming your intention to work together towards a more balanced and supportive internal dialogue.

The next two pages are blank, designed to suit the writing dialog.

Use this page for the dialog with your Inner Critic.

_____

_____

_____

_____

_____

_____

_____

_____

_____

_____

_____

_____

_____

_____

_____

_____

_____

_____

_____

_____

_____

_____

_____

_____

_____

_____

_____

_____

_____

_____

_____

_____

Use this page for the dialog with your Inner Critic.

_____

_____

_____

_____

_____

_____

_____

_____

_____

_____

_____

_____

_____

_____

_____

_____

_____

_____

_____

_____

_____

_____

_____

_____

_____

_____

_____

_____

_____

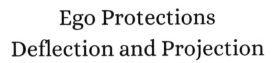

Ego Protections
Deflection and Projection

Deflection, as a psychological process, is a defense mechanism that involves redirecting blame, responsibility, or negative attention away from oneself and onto others or external circumstances. The Ego uses this strategy to avoid facing personal accountability, uncomfortable emotions, or acknowledging own flaws and mistakes.

Deflection might involve shifting the focus of a discussion to unrelated matters or the actions of others. By doing so, individuals create a diversion that distracts from their own role in a situation.

Common signs of deflection include evasive language, denial of personal involvement, and pointing out the faults of others.

Projection, on the other hand, involves attributing one's own thoughts, feelings, desires, or characteristics to others. It occurs when an individual unconsciously denies these aspects within themselves and instead perceives them in the people around them. This defense mechanism serves as a way to protect one's self-image by displacing inner conflicts or insecurities onto external targets.

In projection, individuals may find it challenging to acknowledge or accept certain emotions or traits within themselves due to fear, shame, or discomfort. As a result, they project these feelings onto others, often without realizing they are doing so. For instance, someone who struggles with feelings of jealousy might project those feelings onto a friend by accusing them of being envious.

Becoming more aware of how you deflect or project can help you understand what your ego wants to avoid. From there, you will more easily see what you have pun into your Shadow.

Deflection

It's important to know that we all make deflections. They are a natural response of the ego, when faced with something it doesn't want to acknowledge.

To become aware of the ways you avoid responsibility, shift blame or focus to others, answer these questions.

How do I react when someone criticizes me or points out my flaws?

_____

_____

_____

_____

_____

Have I ever shifted blame onto someone else when faced with criticism? Explain the situation in short.

_____

_____

_____

_____

_____

Have I ever witnessed someone else attempting to shift the blame onto me or another person? How did it make me feel? How did I react?

_____

_____

_____

_____

_____

Deflection
Journaling

When have I avoided taking responsibility for my actions by blaming others or shifting the focus of the conversation to the other participant?

What was my reason behind it? What was I avoiding by shiting blame/focus? What does this say about my shadow?

Projection Exercise

Projections are another frequent defense mechanism for avoiding awareness. You can do this exercise to understand what you might be projecting into others.

1. Sit comfortably and close your eyes. Visualize a made-up person that would be the total opposite of you.

2. Start with the physical attributes, and do them with as much detailing as possible.

3. Then, describe this person. Give it the opposite mindset, thoughts, personality traits, and behaviors from the ones you're prone to.

4. Lastly, draw a picture of the imagined person, and write the main aspects down.

These are the most often projections you might be "labeling" others with.

Projection
Journaling

When have I projected something onto others without having definitive proof about being right?

What exactly did I project? Do I identify with the opposing personality trait/emotion/behavior? What does this say about my shadow?

_____
_____
_____
_____
_____
_____
_____
_____
_____
_____
_____
_____
_____
_____
_____
_____
_____
_____
_____
_____
_____
_____
_____

The Things that Shaped Me

Our development is deeply interconnected with external influences, surrounded by a vast tapestry of experiences, relationships, and events. Other people and the events we encounter play a crucial role in shaping our identity, beliefs, values, and behavior.

Family, caregivers, peers, teachers, and communities are integral to our journey of growing up and developing. Through observation, imitation, and direct communication, we internalize societal norms, cultural values, and social expectations. These relations provide a foundation for our developing sense of self and identity. Both consciously and unconsciously, we align our behaviors and beliefs with those around us, fostering a sense of belonging and integration.

Other people serve as living models from whom we acquire information, behaviors, and attitudes. Even after we've grown, the people that surround us play a role in how we perceive ourselves, others, and the world to be. Often, their perceptions of who we are can cover the ones we have about ourselves, and soon, we start believing we are who they say we are. And yes, this is great when someone thinks you're wonderful, talented, or smart. But what happens when they think you're egoistic, dumb, or incompetent?

The experiences we have also shape how we perceive ourselves, others, or the world to be. The lasting effect of any experience is the conclusion and the consequences we draw from it. So, due to limited experience, our brain might sometimes label things unrightfully simply because they remind us of some other experience.

Whether through conscious or subconscious means, the influence of other people and events acts as a melting pot, molding our character and contributing to our ongoing journey of self-discovery and personal development.

The People that Shaped Me

In the spaces below, write the names of the people who greatly impacted your life, either positively or negatively. Three of the people would have a positive influence, and the other three - a negative one. In the middle column, write the thing you liked about each person. In the last column, write a thing you didn't like about them.

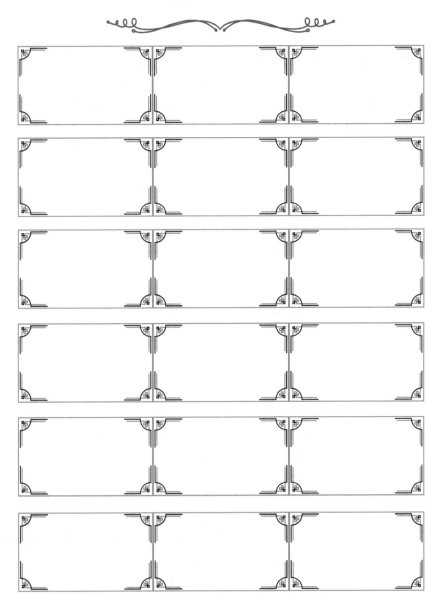

The People that Shaped Me
Exercise

Now, it's time to review your experience with a couple or all of the people you named in the previous exercise. Do so with the help of these guidelines and questions.

1. Close your eyes, and take a few breaths. Find a quiet place where you won't be interrupted and you'll have privacy.
2. First, choose two main people to work with during this exercise. One of them should be connected to a negative experience and the other to a positive one.
3. Start with the person you had a negative experience with. Next, repeat this exercise with the person you've had a positive experience too. If you want, you can repeat the process with all the named people.
4. Start the process by closing your eyes and visualizing that person in front of you. Give them as many details as you can.
5. Next, rewind different situations and experiences you had with them. Focus your attention on:
   - how did this person shape you?
   - what experiences have you two had?
   - how did you feel during those experiences?
   - what came out of those experiences?
   - what conclusions did you draw from those experiences?
   - how did this impact you later in life?
6. Now, start talking to the visualized person in front of you. Tell them about the things you just went over.
7. Once you're done, forgive them for the experience when you talk with the person that you've had a negative experience with. In the second part, when talking with the person you've had a positive experience with, express your gratitude.

The People that Shaped Me
Journaling

Think about the person that you believe had the biggest positive influence on you while you were growing up.

Write down about some of the most memorable experiences, the things you learned from them, and how they made you feel. In the end, express your gratitude and appreciation for everything they did.

_____

_____

_____

_____

_____

_____

_____

_____

_____

_____

_____

_____

_____

_____

_____

_____

_____

_____

_____

_____

_____

_____

The Events that Shaped Me

To start off on your journey of determining the events that shaped you, do the "The timeline of my life" exercise.

Below, you will find an empty line. The left side is a point in time when you were born, and the right side is this present moment.

Take a moment to reflect on your life and the memorable events. These could be milestones, achievements, challenges, relationships, or turning points.

On your timeline, mark with dots some of the memorable experiences in chronological order. If the event was in your childhood - mark it closer to the left. Around the dot, write the year it happened or how old you were. You can also give it a name or short description.

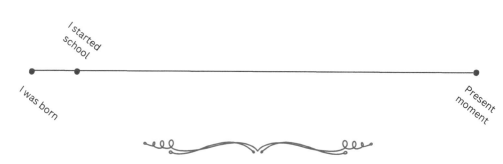

Now, use three different colors to mark the emotions behind each experience. Use one color for positive experiences, another for negative, and a third color for experiences you are indifferent toward.

Color the squares for the corresponding color so you don't forget what each color represents.

| Color for positive events | Color for negative events | Color for indifferent events |

Reflect:

What color predominates your timeline?

What kind of experiences are you prone to remembering?

Do you still hold emotions connected to those experiences?

The Events that Shaped Me
Exercise

Now, choose the one most negative event that shaped you in your life. Take the time to calm and prepare yourself for the work, and then do this exercise step by step.

- Close your eyes and go over this negative experience.

- Reflect on how this event influenced your thoughts and mindset. Consider both short-term and long-term effects.

- Reflect on how this event influenced your feelings and emotional state. Consider both short-term and long-term effects.

- Reflect on how this event influenced your beliefs and outlook on life. Consider both short-term and long-term effects.

- Reflect on how this event influenced your actions. Consider both short-term and long-term effects.

- Reflect on how this event influenced your relationships in the future. Consider both short-term and long-term effects.

- Reflect on any possible fear you might have gained due to this event. How did you act later on to prevent this thing from happening again?

- Whom do you hold accountable for this situation? Have you forgiven whomever you hold accountable? If not, why not? If yes, why?

- Reflect on the lessons you've learned from this experience. What traits have you developed due to it? What abilities?

The Events that Shaped Me
Journaling

Here, write down all the reflections you did during the previous exercise.

Instead of focusing on explaining the situation that happened back then, focus on how you feel right now, and how that experience transfers into your life today.

_____

_____

_____

_____

_____

_____

_____

_____

_____

_____

_____

_____

_____

_____

_____

_____

_____

_____

_____

_____

_____

_____

_____

_____

The Events that Shaped Me
Journaling

Imagine you are writing a letter to your past self just before this significant event occurred. Address your past self with kindness and empathy, offering guidance and insight based on what you know now.

_____

_____

_____

_____

_____

_____

_____

_____

_____

_____

_____

_____

_____

_____

_____

_____

_____

_____

_____

_____

_____

_____

My Triggers

Triggers are stimuli, situations, or experiences that evoke strong emotional responses or psychological reactions due to their association with past memories, traumas, or deeply held beliefs. Triggers can range from specific words or images to places, people, or events. When encountered, triggers can lead to heightened anxiety, fear, anger, sadness, or other intense emotions.

Identify one specific trigger that tends to evoke strong emotional reactions or discomfort. It could be a word, a situation, a place, or an event.

_____

_____

_____

_____

_____

Reflect on the origin of this trigger. Can you recall the earliest memory or event that might have created this association? Include details about what happened, your emotional state at the time, and any significant people involved. If you can't find a particular memory, focus on how this affected you sometimes in the past.

_____

_____

_____

_____

_____

Continues on the next page...

My Triggers

Describe the emotional response the trigger evokes in you. Is it fear, anger, sadness, or something else?

_____

_____

_____

_____

_____

Write down the physical sensations you experience when encountering the trigger. Pay attention to your body's signals.

_____

_____

_____

_____

_____

Document the thoughts that arise when the trigger is activated. Are there specific beliefs, assumptions, or self-talk that contribute to your emotional reaction?

_____

_____

_____

_____

_____

My Triggers
Exercise

Here is an exercise you can do to find coping strategies for your trigger.

- Sit comfortably in a quiet room where you won't be distracted.

- Take a few deep breaths and imagine a situation where you are triggered. It can be an imaginary situation or a real one you can remember.

- Take a second and think about healthy coping strategies you can use when faced with this trigger. These could include deep breathing, grounding techniques, positive self-talk, or seeking support from a trusted friend.

- Reflect on past instances when you successfully managed this trigger. What strategies did you employ, and how did they help you navigate the situation?

- Say an affirmation or a positive statement that you can use to counteract the negative impact of this trigger. For example, "I am in control of my reactions and emotions."

- Reflect on your capacity for growth and resilience. Consider how working through this trigger contributes to your emotional well-being or everyday life.

- Visualize your emotional state being unaffected by the trigger. Imagine the trigger happening to you and you not having an emotional reaction to it. How does it feel? What emotions would you have in that situation?

- Use the journaling section on the next page to write the findings from this exercise. Visit that page regularly to remind yourself about the steps you can take to work through the trigger.

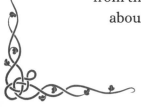

My Triggers
Journaling

Write down the awarenesses you gained during the previous exercise.
- name healthy coping strategies for your trigger
- recall a situation where you were successful at managing the trigger
- come up with positive affirmations you can use to center yourself
- write about the positive benefits it will bring you
- write about the emotional state of getting over that trigger.

_____

_____

_____

_____

_____

_____

_____

_____

_____

_____

_____

_____

_____

_____

_____

_____

_____

_____

_____

_____

Chapter II
Polarities and Finding Balance

Balancing various aspects of our lives, from work and relationships to self-care and personal growth, is not merely a luxury but a fundamental necessity for overall well-being.

Life is a delicate scale, with different facets of our existence on either side. When one area tips too heavily, it not only affects that particular aspect but ripples into others as well. Neglecting self-care, for instance, might lead to burnout and diminished productivity at work. Conversely, over-prioritizing career ambitions could strain relationships and compromise mental and physical health.

Shadow work especially dives into the aspect of balance. Striving for balance ensures that each dimension receives the attention it deserves, fostering holistic well-being.

Balancing life is not about rigidly dividing time but about mindful choices and setting priorities. It requires self-awareness to recognize when one area is overpowering the rest. Strategies like time management, setting boundaries, and embracing mindfulness practices can help regain equilibrium.

In Shadow work, balance is found through the awareness of the conflicts we are faced with and the choices we have to improve our situation. This chapter will dive into balance in personality traits, polarities, professional life, and the contact we make with people.

In this fast-paced world, the quest for balance might seem challenging. However, the rewards of a well-balanced life are abundant: increased happiness, enhanced relationships, improved mental and emotional health, and a more profound sense of purpose.

Finding Balance
Exercise

This exercise encourages you to practice physical and mental balance by incorporating mindfulness into a simple activity - walking.

- Find a peaceful outdoor location where you can walk without distractions. It could be a park, a trail, or even a quiet street.

- Begin your walk at a comfortable, leisurely pace. Take a few deep breaths to center yourself and start walking.

- Focus your attention on all sensations - how you make each step, how you hold yourself, what happens around you, how you feel, and what thoughts come to mind.

- After a few minutes of mindful walking, pause and stand on one foot. Lift your right foot off the ground and balance on your left foot for about 10-15 seconds.

- Lower your right foot and switch to balancing on your right foot for the same duration.

- Resume walking at a slow pace and continue to focus on the sensation of each step.

- As you walk, reflect on the concept of balance in your life. Are there areas that feel out of balance? Are there ways you can create more equilibrium between different aspects of your life?

- As you conclude your mindful walk, take a few moments to express gratitude for the balance in your life, both the achieved and the ongoing journey.

You will have the opportunity to reflect on this experience on the next page.

Finding Balance
Journaling

Reflect on the exercise you just did. Take your time to organize your thoughts and write about your experience. Mention the sensations you became aware of, how you felt and what you thought.

Lastly, dedicate some time to reflect on the balance you think you have, or don't have, in your life.

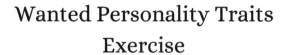

Wanted Personality Traits
Exercise

Here is an exercise to do to reinforce your wanted personality traits.
To do this exercise, start with one personality trait and follow all the instructions to the last one. Then, choose another personality trait and go over it once more. Repeat the process with as many personality traits as you can think of.
To not lose track of thought, we recommend you take short notes.

- Begin by listing one personality trait that you admire or consider positive. It could be a quality you see in role models, friends, or people you look up to. Then add a reason why you believe that personality trait is important.

- Consider the impact of this trait on your life satisfaction, relationships, and overall well-being.

- Reflect on a situation where you portrayed this personality trait.

- Identify contexts where you naturally exhibit the wanted trait. What circumstances provoke you to display this positive personality trait?

- Reflect on a situation where you could have portrayed this personality trait, but you didn't. What exactly stopped you?

- Set specific goals for cultivating this positive trait. How can you practice this personality trait in your everyday life?

- What is the opposite personality trait of this one?

- Reflect on a situation where you portrayed this opposite personality trait.

- What circumstances provoke you to display this opposite personality trait?

Unwanted Personality Traits
Exercise

Now, it's time to dive a little deeper into the personality traits you don't like about yourself.

Start with one personality trait and follow all the instructions to the last one. Then, choose another personality trait and go over it once more. Repeat the process with as many personality traits as you can think of.

Approach this exercise with self-compassion, recognizing that personal growth is a gradual process.

- Begin by listing one personality trait that you find problematic or that lead to negative outcomes in your life. Then add a reason why you believe that personality trait is negative or unwanted.

- Consider the impact of this trait on your life satisfaction, relationships, and overall well-being.

- Do you find that certain unwanted traits emerge more strongly in specific relationships, situations, or emotional states? What might trigger these behaviors?

- Reflect on a situation where you portrayed this personality trait.

- What circumstances provoke you to display this unwanted personality trait? Is it okay, in those situations, to display that personality trait?

- When you exhibit these unwanted traits, how do you usually feel afterward? Do you experience regret, guilt, or a sense of discord within yourself?

- Can you trace back to any childhood experiences, past events, or influences that might have contributed to the development of these unwanted traits?

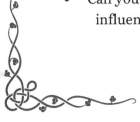

Wanted VS. Unwanted
Personality Traits
Journaling

Based on your reflections, set specific goals for cultivating wanted traits and minimizing unwanted ones. Write down actionable steps you can take to embody these changes.

You can break down these goals into short-term and long-term objectives. Consider how you can integrate these changes into your daily life.

Anima VS. Animus

The concepts of the Anima and the Animus are vital parts of Jungian analytical psychoanalysis. They represent the unconscious aspects that exist within the psyche of every individual, regardless of gender.

The anima is a complex archetype that symbolizes the unconscious feminine qualities and energies that counterbalance the conscious masculine elements in men. Conversely, in women, it is the animus that holds the unconscious masculine qualities and energies that balance out the conscious feminine ones.

The Anima and the Animus take various forms in dreams, fantasies, and projections. They can manifest as both positive and negative figures, reflecting different emotional and psychological states.

Positive Anima manifestations, for example, may bring about inspiration, creativity, and a sense of connection. Negative Anima can lead to irrational emotions, mood swings, and chaotic behavior if left unacknowledged.

Similarly, positive animus manifestations can inspire rational thinking, assertiveness, and protective behaviors. However, the negative animus can lead to dogmatic beliefs, rigidity, and aggression when not acknowledged.

The Anima and the Animus act as a bridge between the conscious ego and the unconscious, helping to integrate suppressed or neglected aspects of the self. If not made conscious, they can easily be projected onto others, especially people of the opposite sex. With that, they can greatly impact relationships.

Anima VS. Animus

To familiarize yourself with what your Anima and Animus hold, answer these questions.

In my experience, positive qualities, emotions and traits of women are

_____

_____

_____

_____

_____

In my experience, negative qualities, emotions and traits of women are

_____

_____

_____

_____

_____

In my experience, positive qualities, emotions and traits of men are

_____

_____

_____

_____

In my experience, negative qualities, emotions and traits of men are

_____

_____

_____

_____

Anima VS. Animus
Exercise

This exercise aims to help you become conscious of the anima (for males) or the animus (for females).

For this exercise, you would need to include the qualities you mentioned on the previous page. You can either move back and forth between pages or rewrite the answers on another piece of paper while staying on this page for the exercise.

- Set aside dedicated time in a quiet and comfortable space where you won't be interrupted.

- Acknowledge your intention to explore and connect with your inner anima (for males) or animus (for females). Center yourself with a few deep breaths.

- Depending on the sex, you would be dedicating time and effort to the qualities, emotions, and traits of the opposite sex.
- If you are male, focus on the Anima (the female qualities you mentioned); if you are female, focus on the Animus (male qualities you mentioned).

- Read through the positive qualities, emotions, and traits you named. How many of them do you recognize in yourself? This is what your positive Anima/Animus is made out of.

- Read through the negative qualities, emotions, and traits you named. How many of them do you recognize in yourself? Chances are - you will say yes to very few, if any. Think about a situation where you portrayed each of these qualities. This is your negative Anima/Animus.

On the next page, you will have a chance to reflect on this exercise through journaling.

Anima VS. Animus
Journaling

After the exercise, take a moment to reflect on your experience. What insights, emotions, or realizations emerged during your exploration? Focus your attention on the negative Anima/Animus.

Consider how the qualities of your inner negative anima/animus interact with your daily life and relationships. Do you tend to project them onto people of the opposite sex? Do you avoid portraying or showing these qualities, emotions, or traits at all costs?

_____
_____
_____
_____
_____
_____
_____
_____
_____
_____
_____
_____
_____
_____
_____
_____
_____
_____
_____
_____
_____

Professional VS. Private Life

Managing and balancing between work and private life can be a hard thing to do in todays society. Managing the roles, the responsibilities and the communication styles seems to be one of the hardest things to do.

Often, two unbalanced things happen - people either forget that they've left work and act in the same way at home; or, they turn a complete opposite of what they do at work during private hours.

What type of person am I at work? What personality traits and emotions do I show there?

_____

_____

_____

What type of person am I at home? What personality traits and emotions do I show there?

_____

_____

_____

Below, there are two circles that intersect. On the left, write the things you are at work, and on the right, the ones you're at home. Use the middle section to write the things that are present in both.

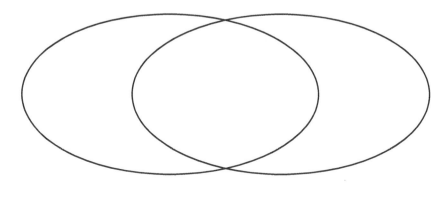

Professional VS. Private Life Journaling

Reflect and consider how your professional and personal life are similar or different. Try thinking through and identifying ways in which you might be acting like a professional at home or acting unprofessionally at work.

How is this transference happening? In what ways are work and home similar, so you transfer personality traits, communication patterns, or emotions from one to the other?

_____

_____

_____

_____

_____

_____

_____

_____

_____

_____

_____

_____

_____

_____

_____

_____

_____

_____

My Needs VS. The Needs of Others

This exercise is designed to help you develop awareness and strategies for balancing your personal needs with the needs of others in a healthy and harmonious way.

- Take some quiet time to reflect on your own needs, desires, and priorities. What activities, self-care practices, and goals are essential for your well-being? Write these down on a piece of paper.

- Consider the most important and close people in your life – family, friends, colleagues, or partners. What are their needs, challenges, and concerns? Write these down, too.

- Look for areas where your personal needs and the needs of others intersect. For instance, do you have shared goals or interests with friends or family members?

- Evaluate how much time and energy you dedicate to meeting your personal needs and how much you allocate to addressing the needs of others.

To make it easier, divide 100% between these two. Are you happy with the numbers, or do you feel it needs adjustment?

- For each personal need, consider how you can communicate your boundaries to others. Let them know when you need dedicated time for yourself.

- Similarly, think about how to initiate conversations about addressing others' needs without neglecting your own.

- Make it a habit to regularly check in with yourself. Are you maintaining a healthy balance between personal needs and the needs of others?

My Needs VS. The Needs of Others
Journaling

Reflect on your experiences with fulfilling your needs versus those of the people around you. Do you have healthy boundaries? If not, how did that happen? If yes, how do you maintain them? Do people take you for granted? Does your behavior remind you of the behavior of your parents?

_____

_____
_____
_____
_____
_____
_____
_____
_____
_____
_____
_____
_____
_____
_____
_____
_____
_____
_____
_____
_____
_____

Introverted VS. Extraverted

Introversion and extraversion are core dimensions of personality that shape how individuals engage with the world, interact with others, and recharge their energy. These terms were popularized by Carl Jung, as he believed that people can be broadly divided into these two tendencies.

Introverts tend to draw their energy from within, often finding beauty in solitary activities. They may feel more energized after spending time alone and delving into their inner thoughts. Introverts are known for their reflective nature, preferring deep conversations and close connections. They may be great for tasks that require focused attention and careful analysis and might get drained in big social gatherings.

Extraverts, on the other hand, thrive on external stimulation and interaction. They gain energy from social interactions, enjoy the company of others, and participate in lively conversations. Extraverts often show enthusiasm and assertiveness and seek new, unknown experiences. They may be great in open environments filled with people and excel in roles that require communication and collaboration.

It's important to note that these two concepts are tendencies, i.e., we all have both of them. People can display different tendencies in various situations and contexts. Yet again, some of us prefer to dwell in our own personal world, while others enjoy spending time with others more.

Embracing the diversity of introversion and extraversion between people, but also within ourselves, can enrich our interactions, increase self-awareness and promote understanding.

Introverted VS. Extraverted Exercise

This exercise aims to help you develop strategies and awareness to find a harmonious balance between your introverted and extraverted tendencies.

- Set aside quiet time for introspection. Relax and take a few deep breaths before you start.

- Reflect on situations or settings where you naturally lean towards introversion or extraversion.

- Take a few deep breaths and try to bring yourself into a state of introversion. To do this easily, you can imagine yourself reading a book or sitting on your balcony alone.

How does it feel?
What is positive about this tendency?
What is negative about this tendency?
When you're ready, open your eyes and reflect for a while on the experience.

- Next, take a few deep breaths and try to bring yourself into a state of extraversion. Imagine yourself being outside with friends and acquaintances at some sort of party or social gathering.

How does it feel?
What is positive about this tendency?
What is negative about this tendency?
When you're ready, open your eyes and reflect for a while on the experience.

- Now, ask yourself these questions:
Which of the two comes more naturally to me?
In what ways can I bring myself closer to balance between the two?
What skills do I need to develop the other tendency?

Introverted VS. Extroverted

Recall one situation where you were introverted and another where you were extraverted. Explain the situations in short and reflect on what made you that way in that particular situation. Was it your own mood or external circumstances? If you could choose, would you prefer to be introverted or extraverted? How can you achieve what you want? How can you bring balance between the two?

_____

_____
_____
_____
_____
_____
_____
_____
_____
_____
_____
_____
_____
_____
_____
_____
_____
_____
_____

What do I need more of?
Exercise

This is an exercise you can do to determine what is lacking out of your life, or you need increased amounts of. Those can be personality traits, emotions, behaviors, situations or anything else.

- Close your eyes and relax. Take a few breaths and try to visualize yourself as you're seeing yourself from the side. DO as much detail as you can connected to the physical appearance.

- Once you have the picture in your mind, briefly explain the person you see in front of you. What's the name of this person? How old is this person? What does she/he do?

- Now, answer these questions for "that" person. Answer them aloud, as if you're saying the answers to the person you visualize.

What personality traits does this person need more of?

What emotional states does this person need more of?

What thoughts does this person need more of?

What behaviors does this person need more of?

What activities does this person need more of?

What self-care does this person need more of?

What moods does this person need more of?

What material things does this person need more of?

What kinds of people does this person need more of?

You can journal on the awareness you came to on the next page.

What do I need more of?
Journaling

Reflect on the things you mentioned during the previous exercise for a while and try to determine how you got to the point of not having those things. How can you increase their presence? What kinds of circumstances would you need to get more of those things? How can you make those circumstances for yourself? Is there anyone that can help you with that?

What do I need less of?

To evaluate what might be an excess in your life right now, answer these questions.

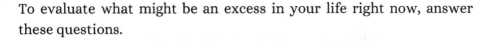

What emotional state do I need less of? How is this excess affecting my well-being, relationships, and overall happiness? What might be the root causes of this excess?

_____

_____

_____

What behavior do I need less of? How is this excess affecting my well-being, relationships, and overall happiness? What might be the root causes of this excess?

_____

_____

_____

What activity do I need less of? How is this excess affecting my well-being, relationships, and overall happiness? What might be the root causes of this excess?

_____

_____

_____

What thought do I need less of? How is this excess affecting my well-being, relationships, and overall happiness? What might be the root causes of this excess?

_____

_____

_____

What do I need less of?
Journaling

Reflect for a while on the answers you gave in the previous page. Choose one thing have excess in and focus on that one.

Through journaling, share briefly what motivated to choose this one. How does it affect you and the people around you? Once you explain why you need less of that thing, think through and come up with a plan and a guide to release yourself from it.

_____

_____

_____

_____

_____

_____

_____

_____

_____

_____

_____

_____

_____

_____

_____

_____

_____

_____

_____

_____

_____

_____

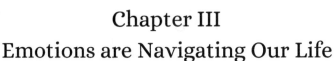

Chapter III
Emotions are Navigating Our Life

Emotions are powerful currents that arise and flow within us, often navigating and guiding our lives. Beyond their fleeting nature, emotions play a profound role in shaping our experiences, decisions, and interactions. They serve as our compass, steering us through life's complex terrain and helping us make sense of the world around us.

Emotions are not just spontaneous bursts of feeling; they are intricate signals from our inner selves. They provide insights into our needs, desires, and values. For instance, the surge of joy when achieving a goal highlights our sense of accomplishment, while feelings of unease in certain situations may signal a misalignment between our values and actions.

Emotions, however, are not without challenges. Navigating them requires self-awareness and emotional intelligence. Often, is very hard to "find our way" around emotions, especially if they are negative, and we, our close surroundings, the people around us, or our society disapprove, disregard, or avoid them. Denying or suppressing emotions can lead to internal conflict and hinder growth. Instead, recognizing and embracing our emotions empowers us to make healthier decisions.

In essence, emotions are the colors that paint the canvas of our lives. They enrich our experiences, enriching the tapestry of human existence. By allowing ourselves to experience and understand our emotions, we embark on a journey of self-discovery and empowerment.

This is the reason why emotions play such a crucial and integral part in Shadow work.

Judgement

Judgment is an inherent aspect of human psychology that shapes our perceptions, decisions, and interactions. It's the process through which we form opinions and evaluations about people, situations, and ideas.

At its core, judgment is a cognitive shortcut that allows us to process information efficiently. Our brains are constantly bombarded with an overwhelming amount of stimuli, and judgment helps us quickly categorize and make sense of this input.

However, this mental efficiency comes with a catch. Our judgments are influenced by cognitive biases—mental shortcuts that can lead to systematic errors in thinking. Confirmation bias, for instance, makes us more likely to seek out information that confirms our existing beliefs, while the halo effect causes us to generalize positive attributes from one aspect of a person to their overall character.

With that, we are often subjected to cognitive biases when explaining the world around us. Hearing something say a sentence that our mean co-worker said might cause us to project all the negative traits of our co-worker to this new person we're just meeting.

Social psychology further reveals that judgment is intertwined with our need for social belonging. We often compare ourselves to others as a way of assessing our own worth, which can fuel judgment. While it helps us navigate life swiftly, unchecked judgment can lead to stereotyping, prejudice, and misunderstanding.

Last but not least, we also self-judge. This is the aspect of reevaluating our own decisions, thoughts, or emotions, leading to feelings of guilt, shame, or self-loathing. Because these emotions are hard to put up, we might be pushing them out to the Shadow, coupled with our natural tendency to judge.

Judgement
Exercise

Here is an exercise you can do to get in touch with your judgement and get closer with this experience within you.

- Choose a comfortable and quiet space where you can reflect without distractions. Close your eyes and take a few deep breaths.

- Try to visualize the emotion of judgment in front of you. How would it look? What color would it have? What material? How big would it be? How would it feel if you touched it? Give it as many attributes as you can.

- From there, think about a recent situation where you found yourself making judgments about someone, whether it's a friend, colleague, family member, or even a stranger. Answer these questions:

- Recall the emotions you felt during that situation. Were you critical, annoyed, frustrated, superior, or dismissive?

- Delve deeper into your thoughts during that moment. What were the specific judgments you made? What assumptions or beliefs did you hold about the person or situation?

- Challenge your own judgments. What evidence did you have to support these judgments?

- Could there be other factors influencing the person's behavior or choices that you're not aware of?

- Have you ever been in a similar situation? How did you feel then? Were you judging yourself in the same way you were judging this other person?

Judgement

Here are some questions to answer to gain awareness of your relationship with judgement.

Write down 5 personality traits that you judge.

_____

_____

_____

_____

_____

Write down 5 emotions that you judge.

_____

_____

_____

_____

_____

Write down 5 behaviors that you judge.

_____

_____

_____

_____

_____

Do you recognize any of these things in yourself?

_____

_____

_____

_____

_____

Judgement
Journaling

Reflect on what you judge yourself for. Which personality traits, emotions, or behaviors do you condemn in yourself? What do you believe is so wrong about those things? Where does this condemnation come from? Is there a situation where these things would be right and okay?

_____

_____

_____

_____

_____

_____

_____

_____

_____

_____

_____

_____

_____

_____

_____

_____

_____

_____

_____

_____

_____

_____

Fear and Avoidance

Fear, a primal emotion hardwired into our psyche, often serves as a signal of potential danger. It's the surge of adrenaline coursing through our veins when faced with the unknown, the uncomfortable, or the uncertain. Yet, fear does not always lead us down a path of brave confrontation. More often than not, it initiates a dance with its close companion: avoidance.

At the core of this intricate psychological interplay lies the principle of self-preservation. Fear, evolutionarily speaking, helped our ancestors survive by alerting them to threats and triggering the fight-or-flight response. Avoidance, then, can be seen as a strategy to maintain safety by steering clear of potentially harmful situations.

Contemporary life introduces a myriad of complex fears—fear of failure, rejection, judgment, and loss. These fears can be paralyzing, and avoidance often becomes a coping mechanism to shield ourselves from the discomfort they bring. Avoiding situations that trigger fear provides temporary relief, but it comes at the cost of personal growth, opportunity, and fulfillment.

When we avoid fearful situations, we inadvertently reinforce the belief that these situations are indeed dangerous. This strengthens the fear response and reinforces the avoidance behavior, creating a feedback loop.

Understanding the psychology behind fear and avoidance allows us to take back control. Instead of being governed by automatic responses, we can choose conscious actions. By acknowledging our fears, questioning their validity, and gradually confronting them, we challenge avoidance and empower growth.

Fear and Avoidance
Exercise

Here is an exercise to get in touch with the sensation of fear. Through the questions, you can identify some of your fears, as well as work through some of the underlying reasons for them.

- Choose a comfortable and quiet space where you can reflect without distractions. Close your eyes and take a few deep breaths.

- Try to visualize the emotion of fear in front of you. How would it look? What color would it have? What material? How big would it be? How would it feel if you touched it? Give it as many attributes as you can.

- Next, try to think of situations, scenarios, or things that you fear. To manage the whole exercise better, take notes on a piece of paper.

- Reflect on why this particular fear exists within you. Has there been a past experience that contributed to it? Are there any underlying beliefs or assumptions that fuel this fear?

- Take a moment to pay attention to your body. How does your body react when you think about this fear?

- How do you feel when confronted with this fear? Are you anxious, stressed, worried, or something else?

- Close your eyes again and visualize yourself facing this fear. Imagine the scenario in detail. What does it look like? How do you feel as you confront it?

Fear and Avoidance

Choose 3 of your biggest fears and write them in the left column. Then, rate each fear from 1 to 5 regarding how rational each fear it. In the last column, write what you do to prevent said fear from becoming a reality. This might include having certain personality traits, and behaviors or avoiding certain situations.

Name the fear	Rationality rating	How I prevent this fear from happening?

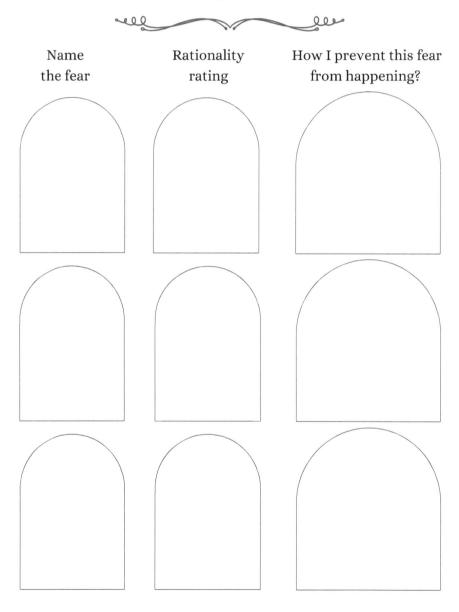

Fear and Avoidance
Journaling

Reflect on your biggest fear. It can be connected to yourself, your future, your loved ones, your career or anything else. Then try to find situations in the past where this fear was close to becoming true. How did you feel back then? What conclusions did you get out of that situation? How has that situation affected your current fear? Are they connected? How?

_____

_____
_____
_____
_____
_____
_____
_____
_____
_____
_____
_____
_____
_____
_____
_____
_____
_____
_____
_____
_____
_____
_____
_____

Hurt and Pain

Emotional pain is something that is an existential truth for all people. These feelings are not only natural but also play a pivotal role in shaping our psychological landscape and influencing our behaviors.

We are faced with hurt and pain whenever our Ego is hurt, when we perceive that an injustice has been made, when we don't get our needs met, or when reality opposes our expectations. When our expectations or needs are unmet, whether in relationships, accomplishments, or self-perception, it can give rise to a range of painful emotions like disappointment, rejection, and sadness.

With the Ego's natural tendency to need and want, pain and hurt are inevitable, as we can't always get the things we want. And since these emotions are hard to bear and most of the time the Ego has a hard time solving them, they often go into the Shadow.

Furthermore, our Shadow might be filled with repressed memories of hurt and pain. This, too, happens due to the inability of the Ego to continue living life "sure of itself" if it's filled with these emotions. They hinder the Ego's need for control as well as the wish to be "strong, right, and well-adjusted to reality."

Repressed or Shadowed hurt and pain don't simply stop existing. Instead, they start guiding our life from the Shadow, as avoidance to similar situations where similar emotions might arise. Plus, they might lead to the unconscious need to hurt the people we believe hurt us.

Avoiding or suppressing pain can lead to prolonged suffering, impacting mental and even physical health. Embracing pain, on the other hand, can foster resilience, growth, and emotional intelligence. Furthermore, it will lead to less avoidance of situations since their negative energy and the remaining power will be drawn out of the Shadow.

Hurt and Pain
Exercise

Here is an exercise to get in touch with unresolved pain and hurt. Through the questions, you can identify some pains and work through some of the underlying reasons for them.

- Choose a comfortable and quiet space where you can reflect without distractions. Close your eyes and take a few deep breaths.

- Try to visualize the emotion of emotional pain in front of you. How would it look? What color would it have? What material? How big would it be? How would it feel if you touched it? Give it as many attributes as you can.

- Next, try to think of situations, scenarios, or things that you feel hurt by. To manage the whole exercise better, take notes on a piece of paper.

- Choose one painful experience you want to work with. Visualize it in front of you and answer these questions:

- What exactly hurt you? Try to put this into one sentence.

- Name all the emotions you felt during the experience.

- Name all the emotions you hold about that experience now. Are the same emotions still active? If not, what were you able to release? How did you achieve that?

- If you could change one thing about this experience - what would that be?

- Now, go to the next page to gain some more awareness about this situation. When you're ready, return to this page to "close the process."

- Close your eyes and visualize the experience moving further and further away from you.

Hurt and Pain

Further develop your awareness of the painful situation through these questions.

Who do you hold accountable for the hurt? Was it a particular person, their actions, or the whole experience?

_____

_____

_____

_____

Did you have any responsibility for the whole experience? What did you do? What could have you done, looking at the whole thing from today's perspective?

_____

_____

_____

_____

What conclusions/beliefs did you get out of the experience?

_____

_____

_____

_____

With what thoughts/emotions/actions do you prevent the same thing from happening? Is that restricting in any way? How?

_____

_____

_____

_____

Hurt and Pain
Journaling

Reflect for a while on the whole experience and then try to come up with alternative scenarios - one worse and one better.

For both of those scenarios, answer these questions: What could have happened differently? How? What would have, then, been the outcome?

_____

_____

_____

_____

_____

_____

_____

_____

_____

_____

_____

_____

_____

_____

_____

_____

_____

_____

Jealousy is often rooted in a sense of threat to a valued relationship or possession. It arises when we fear losing something significant to a perceived rival. Jealousy can fuel feelings of insecurity, possessiveness, and a need for validation.

Envy, on the other hand, revolves around a longing for what others have. It arises when we compare ourselves to someone who appears to possess qualities, achievements, or possessions we desire. Envy is driven by a desire for improvement but can easily turn into bitterness or resentment if not managed.

The psychology of jealousy and envy is often intertwined with self-esteem. Individuals with low self-esteem may be more susceptible to feelings of jealousy or envy as they may perceive others as having more value or worth. Moreover, social comparison plays a significant role in developing feelings of jealousy and envy, especially in today's world of social media and "perfect persona" portrayals.

The way in which these emotions can be incorporated into the Shadow is quite simple. These emotions are socially considered "negative emotions," and people might feel guilt if they feel or express these emotions. So, often, these emotions are pushed into the Shadow, far from the Ego's idea of self-confidence, understanding, and appreciation of others.

One good way to become aware of the Shadowed jealousy or envy is to check for projections. People who tend to often "label" others as jealous or envious usually experience these feelings themselves.

Emotional intelligence and self-knowledge are vital for managing jealousy and envy. Recognizing these emotions without judgment and investigating their root causes can lead to healthier coping mechanisms.

Jealousy
Exercise

This exercise is designed to help you connect with and understand your feelings of jealousy, gain insight into the triggers and underlying emotions, as well as develop strategies to manage it more effectively.

- Choose a comfortable and quiet space where you can reflect without distractions. Close your eyes and take a few deep breaths.

- Try to visualize the emotion of jealousy in front of you. How would it look? What color would it have? What material? How big would it be? How would it feel if you touched it? Give it as many attributes as you can.

- Think of a recent situation where you experienced jealousy.

- To manage the whole exercise better, write your reflections down.

- Recall the details of the situation that triggered your jealousy. What specific event or circumstance caused you to feel this way?

- Reflect on the emotions you experienced during this situation. Were you feeling angry, anxious, insecure, or inadequate?

- Delve into the underlying emotions that might be contributing to your jealousy. Are there feelings of inadequacy, fear of missing out, or a desire for validation?

- Imagine yourself in the other person's shoes. Try to understand their journey, challenges, and hard work that led to their success. How does this perspective change your feelings of jealousy?

- Reflect on the positive aspects of your jealousy. Is there something you can learn from your jealousy? Can it motivate you to set goals or improve certain aspects of your life?

Envy

To get in contact with your envious feelings, answer these questions.

Name 5 people you compare yourself with. They can be from your immediate surroundings or famous people you admire. What aspects do you compare? Are they achievable for you or not?

_____

_____

_____

_____

_____

Name 5 material things that you want to possess.

_____

_____

_____

_____

_____

Name 5 personality traits that you want to possess.

_____

_____

_____

_____

_____

Go over the material things and personality traits you named and ask yourself:

- Is this achievable for me?
- How?
- What can I start doing to get closer?

Jealousy and Envy
Journaling

Reflect on your opinions about jealousy and envy. How do you distinguish them in your life? When are you jealous, and when envoys? Then, recall one situation for both and determine what it is that you were jealous/envious of. Why?

Then, reflect a while on the psychology behind these emotions - when we are jealous or envious, we believe we don't have that thing ourselves, or we fear losing it. How was this true in your situations?

_____
_____
_____
_____
_____
_____
_____
_____
_____
_____
_____
_____
_____
_____
_____
_____
_____
_____
_____

Guilt and Regret

Guilt and regret are integral parts of the human psyche. They are "haunting" emotions that emerge from our past actions and decisions.

Guilt arises when we feel responsible for causing harm or wrongdoing to others, violating our own moral standards. It's often accompanied by a sense of remorse, and its purpose is to motivate us to repair relationships, make amends, and learn from our mistakes.

Regret, on the other hand, centers around decisions we perceive as mistakes or missed opportunities. It stems from the realization that we could have acted differently. Regret can lead to feelings of sadness, disappointment, and a longing for a chance to rewrite the past.

By acknowledging our feelings and accepting responsibility, we can take steps to repair relationships, avoid repeating harmful actions, and learn to make better decisions.

However, excessive guilt and rumination or prolonged regret can become detrimental. Dwelling on these emotions can lead to anxiety and depression, as well as hinder our personal growth.

Sometimes, guilt and regret can become "too hard to bear," especially if the consequences are big and long-lasting. In this scenario, they might fall back into the Shadow. The Ego can then mask its fault by playing always-right, never-made-a-mistake, or someone-else-is-always-to-blame games. If you, or a person you know, is this type, chances are - there are some unresolved emotions of guilt and regret in the Shadow, so the Ego compensates from the other side.

It's essential to find the balance between learning from the past and moving forward with a healthy perspective. This is how the Shadowed emotions of guilt and regret can find their "way out" and be released from the system.

Guilt and Regret
Exercise

This exercise is designed to help you connect with and understand your feelings of guilt and regret. By engaging in this exercise, you can gain insights into the situations and decisions that trigger these emotions.

- Choose a comfortable and quiet space where you can reflect without distractions. Close your eyes and take a few deep breaths.

- Try to visualize the emotion of guilt in front of you. How would it look? What color would it have? What material? How big would it be? How would it feel if you touched it? Give it as many attributes as you can. Then, repeat the exercise, visualizing regret.

- Think of a specific situation or decision in your past that you feel guilty or regretful about. It could be something recent or from further back in time.

- Close your eyes and visualize the situation as vividly as possible. Recall the people, places, and emotions involved. Allow yourself to be present in that moment.

- Reflect on whether you are feeling guilt, regret, or a combination of both. Try to identify the emotions that arise as you revisit the situation.

- Describe what happened, your role in it, and why you feel guilty or regretful. Be honest and specific about your feelings.

- Close your eyes and take a few deep breaths. As you exhale, imagine releasing any lingering guilt or regret. Visualize these emotions dissipating and being replaced by a sense of peace.

Guilt and Regret

Here are a few more questions to answer to gain a deeper insight into the situation you went through during the previous exercise.

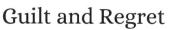

Were there external factors that contributed to your actions or decisions back then? Explain them.

_____

_____

_____

_____

_____

Reflect on what you've learned from this situation. Are there any valuable lessons you can take away from it?

_____

_____

_____

_____

_____

How might you approach a similar situation differently in the future? Write down your intention moving forward. This could be a commitment to learn from your past, practice self-compassion, or take steps to make amends if possible.

_____

_____

_____

_____

_____

Guilt and Regret
Journaling

Reflect on your opinions about guilt and regret. Then, return to the situation you worked on during the previous exercises.

Imagine yourself as an outside observer looking at the situation with empathy. If a friend were in your position, how would you advise them? Extend this empathy to yourself and consider whether forgiveness is warranted. End your journaling with self-forgiveness.

_____

_____

_____

_____

_____

_____

_____

_____

_____

_____

_____

_____

_____

_____

_____

_____

_____

_____

_____

_____

_____

Shame

Shame is another emotion essential for human existence. Nonetheless, it's also one of the most painful and withdrawing emotions out there. Due to its uncomfortability, it's often tucked away in the Shadow, far from awareness and Ego identification.

Shame can shape our self-perception and influence our behavior. This complex emotion carries a heavy psychological weight, stemming from a perceived sense of inadequacy, unworthiness, or moral failure. Almost all of us have some sort of internalized shame, and if not worked through, this emotion can be very silencing for our authenticity.

Shame arises when we believe that our very being is flawed or defective. It's not just about feeling regret for a specific action; it's a broader belief that we are inherently wrong, and there isn't anything that can change that. This emotion is often rooted in early childhood experiences and the messages we receive about our worthiness and acceptability.

The psychology of shame is closely intertwined with self-esteem and self-compassion. While guilt focuses on the behavior ("I did something wrong"), shame focuses on the self ("I am wrong"). This distinction is crucial because shame tends to erode self-esteem and foster self-criticism, making it difficult to cope with challenges and setbacks.

One coping strategy for such a powerful emotion is to push it back into the Shadow. People who tend to think and express highly of themselves, deep down, might be riddled with shame.

While shame can be overwhelming, it's vital to remember that it's not a fixed state. Acknowledging the origins of shame can create space for healing, self-acceptance, and growth.

Shame
Exercise

This exercise is designed to help you connect with and understand your feelings of shame. By engaging in this exercise, you can gain insights into the situations and beliefs that trigger this emotion.

- Choose a comfortable and quiet space where you can reflect without distractions. Close your eyes and take a few deep breaths.

- Try to visualize the emotion of shame in front of you. How would it look? What color would it have? What material? How big would it be? How would it feel if you touched it? Give it as many attributes as you can.

- Think of a specific situation in your past that you feel shame about. It could be something recent or from further back in time.

- Close your eyes and bring the memory to mind. Be gentle with yourself as you explore these feelings. What other emotions do you hold about this shameful experience?

How has this shameful experience affected you later in life? What thoughts/emotions/actions do you avoid just to avoid feeling shame again?

- Close your eyes and visualize yourself releasing the weight of shame. Picture yourself letting go of the shame and embracing a sense of self-worth.

- Consider how you can approach similar situations in the future with self-compassion and understanding.

- Identify one small step you can take to challenge shame in your life. It could be sharing your feelings with a trusted friend, seeking therapy, or practicing self-compassion exercises regularly.

Shame

Here are some questions to answer to reflect on why this specific memory evokes feelings of shame. During this exercise, you can also identify the underlying beliefs and work on them.

- Underneath, there are three boxes. In the ones far left, write down 3 beliefs connected to this experience that added to your feelings of shame.
- In the middle box, write down where you got this belief from. Was it your family, your friends, or society?
- Reflect on each belief and check if you completely agree with it. Write "yes" or "no" in the third box.

To challenge these beliefs, recall at least one situation where each belief wasn't true.

Shame
Journaling

Reflect on your relationship to shame. Are you prone to feeling this emotion or not?

Then, go back to the shameful situation you worked on during the previous exercises. Imagine you are speaking to a dear friend who is experiencing similar feelings of shame. What would you say to them? Now, offer the same kind and compassionate words to yourself. Write down these self-compassionate statements.

_____

_____

_____

_____

_____

_____

_____

_____

_____

_____

_____

_____

_____

_____

_____

_____

_____

_____

_____

_____

_____

_____

Anxiety

At its core, anxiety is an adaptive response to perceived threats. It's the body's natural way of preparing us to confront danger or challenges.

In evolutionary terms, anxiety was vital for our ancestors facing predators or uncertain environments. However, today, this response can be triggered by various situations without the immediate danger our ancestors had. Anxiety can make us feel restless, worried, and on edge, fundamentally triggered to "save" ourselves, even though there isn't any obvious danger around.

The psychology of anxiety involves a dance between our thoughts, emotions, and physiological reactions. Our brains are wired to detect potential threats, real or imagined, and initiate the fight-or-flight response. When anxiety becomes chronic or excessive, it can lead to heightened stress levels, difficulty concentrating, and physical symptoms such as rapid heartbeat, shallow breathing, and even panic attacks.

Negative self-talk, catastrophic thinking, and excessive worry can exacerbate anxiety. Moreover, the fear of experiencing anxiety itself can create a cycle where the fear of feeling anxious fuels more anxiety.

Anxiety can often be a manifestation of the Shadow. Depending on what we are anxious about, those worries can portray what parts of us need healing. Behind social anxiety, for example, there might be an "imposter" syndrome, where we believe we are not good enough and, sooner or later, people will notice that and ridicule or leave us.

Understanding the psychology behind anxiety empowers us to manage its impact on our lives. By identifying and understanding our triggers and the reasons behind them, we can regulate the body's stress response better and, with that - our anxiety.

Anxiety
Exercise

Here is an exercise designed to get you in touch with your anxiety and the situations that trigger it. It can also serve as sort of "exposure" therapy, where you get adjusted to anxious situations through active imagination.

- Choose a comfortable and quiet space where you can reflect without distractions. Close your eyes and take a few deep breaths.

- Try to visualize the sensation of anxiety in front of you. How would it look? What color would it have? What material? How big would it be? How would it feel if you touched it? Give it as many attributes as you can.

- Think of specific situations from your past where you were anxious. Try to come up with as many of them. You can take notes of the situations that come to mind.

- Do all these situations have something in common? What?

- Now, try to mentally "visit" each of these situations, one by one. Position yourself there, re-living the whole experience - recall details, circumstances, and the feelings you had. Once you position yourself into a situation, answer these questions:

- What do I perceive to be a "threat" here?

- Are any outside "circumstances" increasing my anxiety?

- Are any inner "circumstances" increasing my anxiety?

- Is there anything I could do differently to lower my anxiety in a similar future situation?

- Once you answer these questions, take some time between starting the next scenario. Release your emotions by taking a few deep breaths and focusing on something else.

Anxiety

Here are some questions to answer to further understand your anxiety and its triggers. Work with one (the most memorable) anxious memory you found during the previous exercise.

In this situation, what were the triggers for you? If there was one, just focus on that one. If there were more, name them all.

_____

_____

_____

_____

Tune into your body. Are there any physical sensations that arise when you think about the trigger/triggers?

_____

_____

_____

_____

Now, identify the emotions you were feeling in that situation.

_____

_____

_____

_____

Next, identify the thoughts you have in that situation. Were you fueling your anxiety with your thoughts?

_____

_____

_____

_____

_____

Anxiety
Journaling

Imagine speaking to a friend who is experiencing similar anxiety. What words of comfort and support would you offer? Now, provide the same kind and compassionate words to yourself. Write down these self-compassionate statements.

Include as much helpful and constructive advice or an action plan as possible.

Chapter IV
The Inner Child Lives Forever

The concept of the inner child is a psychological construct often used in therapy and self-help. It represents the emotional and psychological experiences of our childhood, which continue to reside within us into adulthood.

This inner aspect carries the memories, emotions, and beliefs we formed during our formative years. It embodies the vulnerable, curious, and playful part of ourselves that we often suppress or overlook in the hustle and bustle of grown-up life.

Our early interactions with caregivers and the world around us shape our attachment styles, self-esteem, and coping mechanisms. Positive experiences can foster a healthy inner child, while trauma or neglect can lead to a wounded inner child.

Even though it might sound weird, we all have "traumas" in our lives, even if it's as simple as play mates not choosing us on the team. Unresolved childhood wounds and unmet needs can continue to impact our emotional well-being and behavior in adulthood. For example, a person with a wounded inner child stemming from childhood rejection may carry a fear of abandonment or struggle with low self-worth in their adult relationships.

Therapeutic approaches like Inner Child Work aim to heal and nurture the inner child. This process involves reconnecting with the emotions and memories of our younger selves, offering them understanding, compassion, and healing.

The significance of the inner child lies in its potential to foster self-acceptance, emotional healing, and personal growth. By reconnecting with this inner aspect, we can address past wounds, release emotional baggage, and nurture our capacity for joy, creativity, and resilience.

The Inner Child Leaves Forever Journaling

Take the time to close your eyes and imagine your inner child. Then, write everything about it - how old it is, how it looks, what it feels, what it thinks, etc. Introduce your inner child in the third person singular.

_____

_____

_____

_____

_____

_____

_____

_____

_____

_____

_____

_____

_____

_____

_____

_____

_____

_____

_____

_____

What is unresolved?
Exercise

Here is an exercise you can do to get in touch with your inner child and understand what you might have lacked as a child.

- Choose a comfortable and quiet space where you can reflect without distractions. Close your eyes and take a few deep breaths.

- Get in touch with your inner child, recalling the details you named in the previous journaling page.

- Begin a gentle and compassionate conversation with your inner child. Imagine sitting down with them and asking how they feel and what they think.

- Ask your inner child these questions:

  - What emotions do you carry?
  - What needs do you have?
  - What are your biggest concerns?
  - What are your biggest fears?
  - What hurtful experiences do you have?
  - What life areas do you need guidance for?
  - Who is your biggest support?
  - Whose approval do you need and want?
  - What mistakes have you made?
  - What worries you about the future?

- As you conclude the conversation, embrace your inner child with love and compassion. Imagine them feeling safe, comforted, and supported.

What is unresolved?

To gain more insight in the things that your inner child carries, answer these questions:

What negative emotions did my inner child face? Which of those emotions are still present?

_____

_____

_____

_____

_____

What pains did my inner child face? Which of those are still active wounds?

_____

_____

_____

_____

_____

What did my inner child blame itself for? Which of those are still active wounds?

_____

_____

_____

_____

_____

What is unresolved?
Exercise

Once you are more aware of your wounded inner child, it's time to offer some understanding, support and guidance.

Use this exercise to engage in a "parental" relationship with your inner child.

- Choose a comfortable and quiet space where you can reflect without distractions. Close your eyes and take a few deep breaths.

- Visualize your inner child sitting in front of you.

- Begin a gentle and compassionate conversation with your inner child.

- Based on what you said as your inner child, offer support and understanding through sentences like "I understand how that made you feel" or "It's okay to feel that way."

- Forgive your younger self for any perceived mistakes or shortcomings.

- Let them know that you are here to protect and support them. As a grown-up, you can give yourself everything that you need.

- Imagine hugging or holding your younger self, providing the love and care they needed at that time.

- Explain to your inner child that everything turns out well. Tell them about your success, the positive things you accomplished, the difficulties you overcame, and the wonderful people you met as you were growing up.

- Moving forward, promise your inner child and commit to practicing self-care and self-compassion. Treat yourself with the same kindness and care you offered to your inner child.

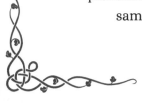

What is unresolved?
Journaling

Now, write a compassionate letter to your inner child.

Share the wisdom and knowledge you've gained as an adult. Offer guidance to your inner child, giving them insights and strategies to navigate their challenges.

Use positive, comforting, and understanding language. Sent out messages that your inner child needed back then. They can include love, support, cheering up, or comforting.

_____

_____

_____

_____

_____

_____

_____

_____

_____

_____

_____

_____

_____

_____

_____

_____

_____

_____

_____

_____

_____

Generational Wounding

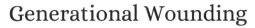

Generational wounding, as a concept, delves into the notion that emotional pain, trauma, and dysfunctional patterns can be passed down through generations.

At its core, generational wounding suggests that unresolved trauma and emotional pain from past generations can affect the psychological well-being and behavior of descendants.

This process is quite logical. Children often internalize their parents' emotional patterns, beliefs, and behaviors. So, unhealed wounds and coping mechanisms are transmitted unconsciously, often through family teachings, dynamics, and behaviors.

Unresolved grief, anger, loss, and unacknowledged emotions are key contributors to generational wounding.
When families suppress or avoid discussing painful experiences, these emotions can become embedded in the family culture, influencing how future generations navigate their own emotions and relationships.
Even if discussed, parents often teach their children to do, avoid, or process things in a certain way. Even though at the base of these actions is the need to protect their children, parents can sometimes "push" their agenda, even though it doesn't align with the time the child is living in or with their needs, wishes, or personal experiences.

Understanding generational wounding is not about assigning blame but rather about recognizing the patterns and working to break the cycle. Therapy and self-awareness play essential roles in healing generational wounds.

By exploring family dynamics, acknowledging the pain, and developing healthier coping strategies, individuals can begin to untangle themselves from the grip of inherited emotional pain.

Generational Wounding
Journaling

Reflect on your childhood. Is there any bigger family trauma that your family suffered? Were there any painful stories that you parents or grandparents told? What message did they portrayed? What lessons did you get out of those stories? How has that experience shaped you? What did you do in your life in accordance with said lessons? What did you avoid in the process?

_____

_____

_____

_____

_____

_____

_____

_____

_____

_____

_____

_____

_____

_____

_____

_____

_____

_____

_____

What have my parents taught me?
Exercise

Here is an exercise to get in touch with your family's energy and what you were surrounded by when growing up.

- Choose a comfortable and quiet space where you can reflect without distractions. Close your eyes and take a few deep breaths.

- Recall the inner child that you got in touch with earlier in this workbook.

- Once ready, also imagine your parents or caregivers around you. *This exercise will work best if you work with one parent at a time.

- Choose one and answer these questions:

- If your parent was an animal - what animal would he/she be?
- If you were describing your parent with one word - what word would it be?
- What do I most vividly remember about this person?
- What thoughts come to mind when I think about this person?
- What emotions come up as I think about this person?
- What has this person taught me?
- How does this person show love and affection?
- How do I show love and affection to this person?

- Once you answer these questions, stop for a second and try to come up with a sentence that you would like to say to this person. It might be expressing an emotion, a thought, advice, or anything else.

- Then, say to them what came to mind. Express everything you need to "tell" to this person but are not able to do in real life.

- Take a few minutes to release the emotions and then repeat the process with the other parent.

What have my parents taught me?

Answer these questions to better understand the influence your parents or caregivers had on you.

What personality traits have I learned from my family?

_____
_____
_____
_____

What emotional reactions have I learned from my family?

_____
_____
_____
_____

What behaviors have I learned from my family?

_____
_____
_____
_____

What beliefs have I learned from my family?

_____
_____
_____
_____
_____

What have my parents taught me?
Exercise

This exercise will help you dive deeper into the things you like and dislike about your parents.

- Choose a comfortable and quiet space where you can reflect without distractions. Close your eyes and take a few deep breaths.

- Imagine your parents in front of you. First, work with one of the parents, then move to the other one.

- To have a smooth flow during the exercise, it might be best to write your answers down and take notes.

- Answer these questions:

- What personality traits do I like in this person?
- What emotional reactions do I like in this person?
- What behaviors do I like in this person?
- What personality traits do I dislike in this person?
- What emotional reactions do I dislike in this person?
- What behaviors do I dislike in this person?
- Which of the traits/emotional reactions/behaviors do I recognize in myself?
- Which of the traits/emotional reactions/behaviors do I strongly oppose and avoid having? What do I do instead?

- Once you answer all the questions, close your eyes, envision your parent in front of you, and say: "You are imperfect, but I accept you as such."

- On the next page, you will get the chance to reflect on your thoughts on this exercise.

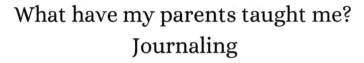

What have my parents taught me?
Journaling

Reflect on your answers from the previous exercise and focus on the extent to which you have the same traits, emotional reactions, and behaviors in yourself.

Which of the likable things do you possess? Which ones you don't but strive to acquire? Why?

Which of the dislikable things do you possess? Which ones do you strongly oppose having and do everything you can to avoid? Why do you do so?

_____

_____

_____

_____

_____

_____

_____

_____

_____

_____

_____

_____

_____

_____

_____

_____

_____

_____

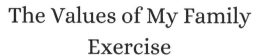

The Values of My Family
Exercise

This exercise can help you understand what values your parents imprinted in you while growing up.

- Choose a comfortable and quiet space where you can reflect without distractions. Close your eyes and take a few deep breaths.

- Close your eyes and think back to your childhood. What values were praised in your family? To get yourself started, answer these questions:
- What was most often discussed in my family?
- What kind of advice did I get from my family regarding:
- social relationships and communication,
- sex and romantic encounters,
- work and career,
- achievement and success,
- money and finances,
- religion or spirituality,
- intellect and knowledge,
- emotions and expressing emotions?

*Write at least one thing that you were taught about each of these topics.

- Reflect on how these values were demonstrated by your family members.
Was it with words, their actions, or decisions?
Were there specific role models or influential figures who embodied these values?

- Try to understand the origins of these values within your family. Were they influenced by cultural, religious, societal, or generational factors? Understanding the context can shed light on their significance.

The Values of My Family

This exercise is made to help you better understand the importance that imprinted values have on you and your life.

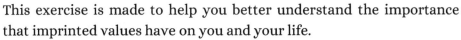

Write down specific sentences, parables, sayings, or moral lessons that your parents often told you to imprint values. (Example - You can't judge a book by its cover.)

Define what value said sentence is portraying.

Now, reevaluate each sentence and rate it from 1 to 5 based on how much you agree with it from today's point of view.

If you rated a particular sentence/saying with a low number, update it. You can adjust it or substitute it with a saying that better reflects your current values.

The Values of My Family
Journaling

Now that you are aware of the values that your family implanted in you, it's important to understand both the positive and the negative aspects of having those values.

How did your familiar values make you a better person? What good consequences have they brought in your life?

What did you have to sacrifice to live in accordance with those values?

_____

_____

_____

_____

_____

_____

_____

_____

_____

_____

_____

_____

_____

_____

_____

_____

_____

_____

_____

_____

What was praised in my family?
Exercise

This exercise is designed to help you develop awareness of the ways your family praised you and your achievements particularly.

- Choose a comfortable and quiet space where you can reflect without distractions. Close your eyes and take a few deep breaths.

- Think back to your childhood. Try to remember instances when you received praise from your family members, such as parents, siblings, or other caregivers. Visualize these moments as clearly as possible.

- Write down the specific words or phrases that were commonly used in the praise you received. Then, answer these questions:
- Was the praise primarily focused on your achievements or your character?
- Were there specific qualities or behaviors that were consistently praised?
- Did the praise tend to be conditional (based on your accomplishments) or unconditional (regardless of what you did)?

- Reflect on how the type of praise you received may have shaped your self-esteem and self-worth.
- Is it achievements or personality traits that you get self-esteem from?
- Is your relationship with self-worth connected to what was praised when you were young?

- Think about your current personal goals and aspirations. Are they aligned with the patterns of praise you experienced in your family, or have you consciously chosen a different path?

What was praised in my family?
Journaling

Reflect for a while on the awareness you came to during the previous exercises. Recognize the positive aspects of the praise you received, such as encouragement and acknowledgment of your strengths.

Also, acknowledge any potential drawbacks, such as excessive pressure or a fear of failure.

What was forbidden in my family? Exercise

This exercise can help you understand the taboo topics in your family while growing up.

- Choose a comfortable and quiet space where you can reflect without distractions. Close your eyes and take a few deep breaths.

- Close your eyes and think back to your childhood. What things were considered taboo, sensitive, forbidden, or off-limits in your family? To get yourself started, answer these questions:
- What was never discussed in my family?
- What kind of advice did I get from my family regarding:
- social relationships and communication,
- sex and romantic encounters,
- work and career,
- achievement and success,
- money and finances,
- religion or spirituality,
- intellect and knowledge,
- emotions and expressing emotions?

*Write at least one thing that was scorned about each topic.

- Reflect on how the disapproval was demonstrated by your family members.
Was it with words, their actions, or decisions?

- Try to understand the origins of this disapproval within your family. Were they influenced by cultural, religious, societal, or generational factors? Understanding the context can shed light on their significance.

What was forbidden in my family?
Exercise

Now, it's time to dive into one particular taboo that hindered your spontanious expression.

- Choose a comfortable and quiet space where you can reflect without distractions. Close your eyes and take a few deep breaths.

- Bring back memories from your childhood when you felt like something was being hidden, unexpressed, or ignored. If you identified more taboos during the previous exercise, focus on just one - the most prominent one.

- Define the topic it was connected with.

- Recall the emotions that were "floating in the air" about said thing.

- Was this taboo a one-time occasion, or was it an ongoing tendency?

- What conclusions did you get out of this experience? What did you learn from it?

- What kind of beliefs have you adopted about the topic?

- What kind of emotions did you have about this topic?

- Is this topic still a taboo for you? Do you have a hard time when this life aspect is in question?
- If not, how did you manage to move past the taboo and "normalize" the aspects of this area?
- Of yes, how can you challenge the taboo from the past? What steps can you take to start talking and acting in this life area more freely and spontaneously?

What was forbidden in my family?

Use these questions to dive deeper on the influence that familiar taboo and disapproval had on your personality traits and actions.

Write the top 5 disapproved things in your family while growing up. They can be personality traits, thoughts, emotions, or actions.

_____

_____

_____

_____

_____

Reflect on how these taboo topics made you feel in your family environment. Did you feel shame, fear, guilt, or confusion when these topics were raised or discussed?

_____

_____

_____

_____

Do you still hold unresolved emotions or thoughts about these topics? Were there any instances where you sacrificed your needs or wishes, just so you don't do something that is close to these disapproved things?

_____

_____

_____

_____

_____

What was forbidden in my family?
Journaling

Consider how these taboos may have influenced your current beliefs, behaviors, and communication style. Are there ways in which these taboos still affect your relationships and decision-making?

Examine whether these taboo beliefs align with your current values and beliefs. Are there any beliefs you want to challenge or modify?

_____
_____
_____
_____
_____
_____
_____
_____
_____
_____
_____
_____
_____
_____
_____
_____
_____
_____
_____

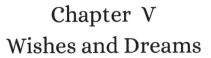

Chapter V
Wishes and Dreams

Wishes and dreams are one of the basic psychological concepts, internal truths for all humans. Beyond the realm of daydreams, they hold profound psychological significance, offering insights into our motivations, aspirations, and the creative power of the mind.

From a young age, we engage in imaginative play and create fantastical scenarios. Psychologists believe this is a fundamental aspect of our cognitive development, helping us learn, problem-solve, and explore possibilities. Wishes provide a sense of purpose and direction, inspiring individuals to set goals and work toward a desired future. The mere act of envisioning a goal can boost motivation and perseverance.

In Shadow work, what we wish and fantasize about can help us understand of our strives. Since fantasies and strives are usually things we don't currently have, they can easily stem from the unconscious and from the Shadow of our Ego.

Dreams, on the other hand, play a central role in Shadow work. As Sigmund Freud explained - "The interpretation of dreams is the royal road to a knowledge of the unconscious activities of the mind."
Dreams are the ways in which our unconscious communicates with our conscious mind and sends messages across. Remembering, interpreting, and understanding dreams can be one of the best ways to peek into the content of our Shadow.

Wishes and dreams reflect our values, passions, and self-identity. They provide a window into what truly matters to us, guiding our life choices and priorities. They often stem from our Shadow, so working with them can help us understand the content of our Shadow and our hidden or repressed desires, needs, unresolved emotions or past experiences.

Expectations

Expectations are powerful drivers of our thoughts and behaviors. We have expectations of ourselves, others have expectations of us, and society often sets its own standards.

The expectations we place on ourselves are deeply intertwined with our self-concept, values, and personal goals. They serve as a source of motivation, guiding us toward achievements and personal growth. Expectations shape our self-esteem and self-identity. Meeting or exceeding our own expectations can boost self-worth, while consistent failure to meet them can erode self-confidence. This is why it's essential to have realistic expectations of ourselves.

Our own expectations stretch further than just our life. We often have expectations about other people, just as they have them about us. Furthermore, we often fantasize about our future, giving rise to expectations about what could and should happen in our lives.

Expectations from others, whether from family, friends, colleagues, or society at large, play a significant role in shaping our social interactions and relationships. These external expectations can impact our self-esteem, sense of belonging, and mental health.

People often seek validation and recognition from others, and when these expectations are not met, it can result in feelings of disappointment or inadequacy.

One way to work around expectations is to have healthy boundaries. Healthy relationships involve setting boundaries and communicating expectations. Clear communication is key to avoiding conflicts arising from unmet expectations.

Balancing expectations, whether from oneself or others, is a delicate act that requires self-awareness and effective communication.

Expectations from Others
Exercise

This exercise can help you understand what expectations others have from you and how you feel about those expectations.

- Choose a comfortable and quiet space where you can reflect without distractions. Close your eyes and take a few deep breaths.

- Imagine the most important people in your life around you.

- When ready, start working with each of them. Once you answer all the questions connected to one person, move to another one.

- What expectations does this person have from you? - Write the expectation down.

- Stay with each expectation for a while.
  What physical sensations do you have?
  What emotions do you have?
  What thoughts do you have?

- Is this expectation realistic?

- Do you want to fulfill this expectation or not?

- What will happen if you live up to this expectation? What emotions would you have?

- What will happen if you don't live up to this expectation? What emotions would you have?

- Before moving to the next person and their expectations, take a few deep breaths and try to release current emotions.

Expectations from Others
Journaling

Reflect for a while about everything you answered during the previous exercise. Then, write a "letter" to one person (or more) who holds or has "pushed" their expectations onto you. In the letter, express how you feel about their expectations, if you want to fulfill them, what positive/negative consequences they might have over your well-being, and anything else you might feel.

_____

_____

_____

_____

_____

_____

_____

_____

_____

_____

_____

_____

_____

_____

_____

_____

_____

_____

_____

_____

Expectations from Myself

These questions can help you understand the expectations you have from yourself. From there, you can more easily reevaluate and adjust those expectations.

What do I expect from myself every day?

_____

_____

_____

_____

_____

What do I expect from myself in the next year?

_____

_____

_____

_____

_____

What do I expect to achieve in my life?

_____

_____

_____

_____

_____

Go over each of your expectations on this page and rate them from 1 to 5 based on how feasible and achievable they are.

Expectations from Myself
Journaling

Reflect on the answers you gave during the previous exercise. How do you feel about everything you wrote? Are they realistic? Do you feel excited or worried? Do you expect too much of yourself? Are there any expectations you want to adjust (lower or increase)? How can you do that?

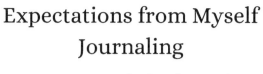

_____

_____

_____

_____

_____

_____

_____

_____

_____

_____

_____

_____

_____

_____

_____

_____

_____

_____

_____

_____

_____

If I could have been anything...
Exercise

This exercise is a visualization. It can help you get in touch with your desires and fantasies about the perfect life.

- Choose a comfortable and quiet space where you can reflect without distractions. Close your eyes and take a few deep breaths.

- Then, visualize what would, for you, be a perfect life. Go into as many details as you can and include aspects like:
  - psychical look
  - personality traits
  - behaviors
  - emotions
  - physical things
  - career
  - achievements
  - people around you
  - experiences

- Take as much time as you need to dive into this visualization. If you like, you can even fantasize about particular situations that can happen if you were to have all that.

- Then, answer these questions:
- What would my thoughts be if this was reality?
- What would I feel if this was reality?
- How would I behave if this was reality?
- What would I think of myself if this was reality?
- What would others think of me if this was reality?

If I could have been anything...

Now, it's time to reflect on the exercise and go deeper into some of the most important aspects.

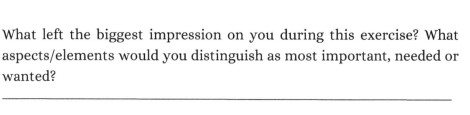

What left the biggest impression on you during this exercise? What aspects/elements would you distinguish as most important, needed or wanted?

_____

_____

_____

_____

_____

Make a drawing of your imagined perfect life. Make sure you include all of the most important aspects in your drawing.

One you're done, take some time to look at this drawing. How do you feel looking at it? What thoughts do you have?

If I could have been anything...
Journaling

Reflect on your exercise and the drawing that came out of it. Then, go over all the aspects you draw. What is their importance? Why do you want those things? Are they achievable with your life as it is right now? Do you currently have them in some form? To what extent? If you don't, what can you do to bring yourself closer to this "perfect" life?

_____

_____

_____

_____

_____

_____

_____

_____

_____

_____

_____

_____

_____

_____

_____

_____

_____

_____

_____

_____

_____

_____

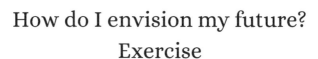

How do I envision my future?
Exercise

The aim of this exercise is to envision your short term and long term goals in order to decide what you want to focus on in the next period of time.

- Choose a comfortable and quiet space where you can reflect without distractions. Close your eyes and take a few deep breaths.

- Begin by taking a few deep breaths to relax your body and mind, focusing on your breath to center yourself.

- Decide whether you want to focus on your short-term future (next 1-3 years) or your long-term future (5-10 years or more). You can do both separately if you wish.

- What are the most important things you want to achieve in the short-term/long-term future? Note any goals, achievements, or experiences that come to mind and write them on a piece of paper.

- Next, rate all written things with a quotation between 1 (low) and 5 (high) based on the following:
- Significance (How important is this goal for me?)
- Feasibility (Is this easily achievable?)
- Time for completion (How long will it take me to achieve this goal?)

- Now, take the time to reflect on your goals and their ratings. To decide your priority goal, answer this question:
- Do I want to do something important, easily achievable, or fast?

- Based on your answer, see which goals align with your current needs. This is the goal you can focus on in the next period of time.

How do I envision my future?

This is an exercise that can help you get in touch with your expectations about future change.

Below, there are 3 columns with 3 rows each. In each of the squares of the first column, write 1 thing you expect to change in the future. Then, fill in the rest of the squares with the answers of the given questions.

What do I expect to change in the future?	How do I expect it to change?	What will be different then?

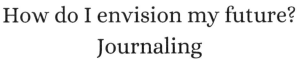

How do I envision my future?
Journaling

Imagine the worst-case scenario for your future. What are your fears for your future? What could go wrong in your life?

Then, reflect on the possibility of these things becoming reality. How much control do you have over this pessimistic fantasy? What could you do to prevent it from becoming a reality? If it happens, how would you cope?

How do I envision my future?
Journaling

Imagine the best-case scenario for your future. What are your hopes for your future? What could be the best possible outcome in your life? Then, reflect on the possibility of these things becoming reality. How much control do you have over this optimistic fantasy? What could you do to encourage it? If it happens, what emotions would you have?

_____
_____
_____
_____
_____
_____
_____
_____
_____
_____
_____
_____
_____
_____
_____
_____
_____
_____
_____

Memorable Dreams

Dreams have fascinated humanity for centuries. While most dreams fleetingly fade from memory upon waking, some leave an indelible mark on our consciousness. These memorable dreams are windows into the enigmatic realm of our subconscious minds.

Memorable dreams are not merely random mental imagery. They often carry emotional weight, vivid imagery, and sometimes even profound messages.

Memorable dreams often involve intense emotions, such as fear, joy, or sadness. These emotions can linger long after waking, making the dream more vivid and unforgettable.

Oftentimes, there are particular symbols, elements, or aspects that might convey some messages that the unconscious wants to communicate with the conscious mind. Memorable dreams might reveal hidden desires or conflicts we're not consciously aware of.

Dreams can also provide us with creative solutions to real-life problems. The brain's problem-solving capacity remains active during sleep, and memorable dreams can provide unexpected answers.

Dreams can also be a mental processing tool, helping us deal with unresolved emotions or trauma.

In theory, there are a few different types of memorable dreams. They include:
Lucid dreams are when we are aware that we are dreaming.
Recurring dreams where the same or similar scenario keeps repeating.
Prophetic dreams in which the dream predicts a future development.
Epic dreams that seem like whole stories, movies, or fantasies.
Nightmares that can portray a negative message, a bad feeling or simply a distressing content.

Memorable Dreams

On this page, you can reflect on your dreams and what they have in common. This can tell you about the things that repeatedly show in your dreams, and ponder upon their meaning.

Most often, I dream about
_____
_____
_____

Most reoccurring themes in my dreams are
_____
_____
_____

Most reoccurring situations in my dreams are
_____
_____
_____

Most reoccurring emotions in my dreams are
_____
_____
_____

Most reoccurring objects in my dreams are
_____
_____
_____

Most reoccurring people in my dreams are
_____
_____
_____

Now, reflect on your answers and understand what is the importance of these things for you. What do they mean to you? What does each thing represent in your mind?

Memorable Dreams
Exercise

This exercise can help you identify one symbol that tends to appear in your dreams.

- Choose a comfortable and quiet space where you can reflect without distractions.

- Begin by taking a few deep breaths to relax your body and mind, focusing on your breath to center yourself.

- Based on your answers on the previous page, what symbol (object, person, emotion, scenario, action, theme) appears in your dreams?

- Make a mental visualization of the symbol. Imagine it in front of you and give it as much detail as possible (material, color, size).

- Stay mentally in touch with said thing and answer:
- What do I think while I'm in "touch" with this symbol?
- What do I feel while I'm in "touch" with this symbol?
- What is the purpose of this symbol?
- If this symbol could talk, what would it say to me?
- If this symbol could listen, what would I say to it?
- What could this symbol teach me?
- If I need to label this symbol, would it be positive or negative?

- When you answer these questions, take a piece of paper and draw a visual representation of the symbol. Depending on its meaning (positive or negative), you can either throw it away as a ritualistic act of "getting rid of it" or you could place it somewhere where you can see and remind yourself of its positive qualities.

- When ready, take a few breaths to center yourself and end the exercise.

Memorable Dreams
Journaling

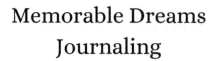

Think about your most memorable dream. It can be a new dream or one that happened some time ago but you still remember vividly.

Briefly describe the dream in the present tense, as if it's happening right now. How do you feel when you describe it?

Then, identify the most important aspects of the dream. They can be objects, actions, situations, people, words, or anything else. Write them down.

Lastly, ponder upon these important elements. What does each of them mean to you? What does each element remind you of? What do you associate it with? How do you feel about each element?

When you put these things together, do they remind you of something else?

_____

_____

_____

_____

_____

_____

_____

_____

_____

_____

_____

_____

_____

_____

_____

_____

_____

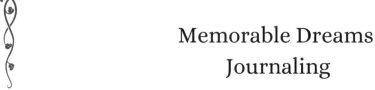

Memorable Dreams
Journaling

Think about a nightmare you had. Describe it in the space below. Use present tense, as if it is happening now. What was the most scary part of the dream? Regardless of how the dream ended, create your own positive or productive ending.

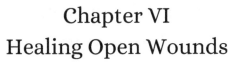

Chapter VI
Healing Open Wounds

Emotional wounds, much like physical ones, have a profound impact on our well-being. These wounds are the result of past experiences, traumas, or losses that have left a lasting mark on our emotional landscape.

Emotional wounds are deep-seated psychological injuries that can persist for years, sometimes even a lifetime if left unaddressed. They can have different backgrounds and hold different negative emotions.

Trauma and traumatic experiences can include abuse, accidents, or violence. Trauma can be divided into "simple trauma" (one-time) and "complex trauma" (recurring).

Unprocessed grief can be another type of wound. This happens in the unfortunate event of losing someone or something important unexpectedly.

Abandonment, betrayal, or rejection can also become open wounds. Unresolved, these issues can lead to long-term difficulties with self-esteem, self-worth, communication, and relationships.

Negative self-perception due to ongoing acts of shaming, ridicule, criticism, gaslighting, or bullying can also be open wounds.

Open wounds can negatively impact physical and emotional well-being, self-esteem, self-worth, and perception of people, the self, and the world. They can also impact relationships and communication.

Note: Due to the complex nature of trauma and the emotions that it might bring if tackled, this chapter won't be asking questions about wounds. Instead, it will focus on activities that one can use to develop healthy coping skills.

Healing Open Wounds
Journaling

Reflect for a while on the theory you read on the previous page.

What are your open wounds? Did something immediately come up in your mind, or did you need to dig deeper to recall something you consider an emotional wound?

What thoughts do you have about this "wound"? What emotions? Are there any ongoing triggers in everyday life that remind you of this "wound" and bring back emotions?

_____

_____
_____
_____
_____
_____
_____
_____
_____
_____
_____
_____
_____
_____
_____
_____
_____
_____
_____

We warmly recommend taking to a therapist to work through unresolved emotional wounds. If not addressed, they might highly impact your physical and mental health, self-perception, and relationships.

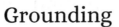

Grounding

In today's fast-paced and often chaotic world, it's easy to feel overwhelmed, anxious, or disconnected from ourselves. Grounding is a practice that offers a way to find stability, calm, and a sense of rootedness in the midst of life's storms. It's a valuable tool for enhancing mental, emotional, and even physical well-being.

Grounding is a mindfulness technique that brings your attention to the present moment, anchoring you in the here and now. It's about reconnecting with your physical body, your senses, and the immediate environment. Grounding can be especially helpful when you feel scattered, stressed, or emotionally overwhelmed.

The aim of grounding is to shift your focus and attention away from racing thoughts, worries about the future, or regrets from the past. Instead, it encourages you to engage your senses, redirecting your attention to the tangible, immediate reality.

Grounding can provide you with a lot of benefits, including reduced stress levels, improved mental clarity, emotional resistance, calmness, and focus, as well as lower the intensity of negative feelings during distressing situations. Grounding can also lower anxiety, connect you with your body and your surroundings, and increase your mental presence in the moment.

In conclusion, grounding is a valuable practice for finding stability and peace in a world that often feels turbulent. Whether you use it as a brief moment of solace in a busy day or as a regular part of your mindfulness routine, grounding offers a path to greater well-being, mental clarity, and emotional resilience.

Grounding
Exercise

This exercise is called the 5-4-3-2-1 exercise and it can help you connect yourself with your body, senses, and surroundings.

This exercise is great for lowering stress and anxiety, lowering the intensity of negative emotions, and distracting yourself from anxious rumination and negative inner talk.

- Choose a comfortable and quiet space where you can reflect without distractions.

- Begin by taking a few deep breaths to relax your body and mind, focusing on your breath to center yourself.

- Then, engage your senses and connect with your surroundings in the following way:
- Find 5 things you can see.
- Lind 4 things you can touch. Touch them.
- Find 3 things you can hear. Take a second to hear each.
- Find 2 things you can smell. Smell them.
- Find 1 thing you can taste. Taste it.

- If you are unable to find enough things for some sense, try imagining something and how it would feel to touch, hear, sell, or taste it.

- In the end, take a few deep breaths and feel your body.

*Note: Once you practice this exercise a few times, you can also do it as a visualization without actually engaging with your surroundings. So, you can imagine how 5 things look, 4 things feel to the touch, how 3 things sound, etc.
This exercise can be great for situations when the surroundings are not appropriate for you moving around and touching, smelling, or tasting things.

Grounding 5-4-3-2-1
Journaling

Reflect on the 5-4-3-2-1 exercise you did on the previous page. How did you feel during the exercise? Were you able to focus on it, or did your mind drift away?

When can you use this exercise in your everyday life? What can this exercise help you with? If possible, come up with particular situations when this exercise can be helpful.

_____

_____
_____
_____
_____
_____
_____
_____
_____
_____
_____
_____
_____
_____
_____
_____
_____
_____
_____
_____
_____

Grounding Body Scan

This exercise can help you get in touch with your body and be aware of all the sensations that happen physically.

This exercise is great for releasing tension and stress from the body. You can use it to calm down in distressing situations, or release the pressure after a hard day.

Start from your toes and work your way up, paying attention to each body part. Notice any tension and consciously release it.

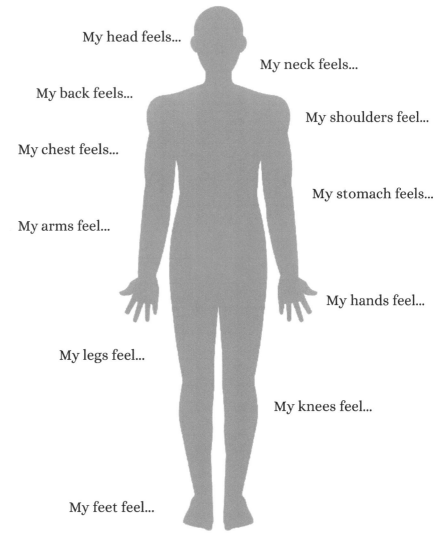

My head feels...

My neck feels...

My back feels...

My shoulders feel...

My chest feels...

My stomach feels...

My arms feel...

My hands feel...

My legs feel...

My knees feel...

My feet feel...

Grounding Body Scan Journaling

Reflect on the Body Scan exercise you did on the previous page. How did you feel during the exercise? Did you have difficulties connecting with a body part? In what body parts were you tensed? Did you manage to release the tension?

When can you use this exercise in your everyday life? What can it help you with? If possible, come up with particular situations when this exercise can be helpful.

_____

_____
_____
_____
_____
_____
_____
_____
_____
_____
_____
_____
_____
_____
_____
_____
_____
_____
_____
_____
_____

Breath

Even though it might sound mundane, breathing is one of the first things we do when we are born and the last thing we do before we die. With it, the act of breathing is one of the most basic things of how we provide ourselves with what we need and how we care for the body.

Since ancient times, different cultures and philosophies have underlined the importance of breathing and breath on physical and mental well-being.

Conscious breathing can be used as a very simple yet very strong way of calming ourselves. In order for the brain to calm, it needs two main things. The first one is to lower rumination and the risk of increasing the intensity of negative emotions through negative thoughts.

The other one is to stay focused and engaged with something in order to maintain concentration on said thing instead of going back to rumination. To find both of these things, you don't have to search further than your breath.

Furthermore, deep diaphragmatic breathing activates the parasympathetic nervous system, which counteracts the stress response. This can reduce the physiological effects of stress, such as increased heart rate and muscle tension.

Observing your breath can heighten emotional awareness. As emotions arise, they often manifest as changes in breathing patterns. Recognizing these shifts can help you understand and address underlying emotional states in everyday situations.

By cultivating awareness of your breath and incorporating intentional breathing practices into your daily life, you can tap into the profound psychological power of each inhale and exhale.

4-5 Breathing
Exercise

This exercise is one of the simplest ones you can do, if you want to release negative emotions and center yourself.

- Find a comfortable and quiet place where you can do this exercise.

- Close your eyes and inhale as you count to 4.

- Then, exhale as you count to 5.

- Repeat as long as you need. You will spontaneously start calming down.

- If you want to further develop this exercise, you can combine it with positive affirmations or visualizations.

- For example, you can visualize negative emotions leaving your body as you exhale and positive emotions flooding you as you inhale.

- In another variation, you can repeat a mantra during inhale, depending on what you need. For example, you might say, "I am calm." Then, as you exhale, you can repeat, "All stress is leaving my body."

- Reflect on the exercise.
Do you find visualizations or mantras more helpful?
How can you incorporated them in your everyday life?

Breath
Journaling

Reflect on the 5-4 exercise you did on the previous page. How did it feel? Were you able to calm and center yourself through breathing? How about including visualizations or positive affirmations?

When can you use this in your everyday life? What can it help you with? If possible, come up with particular situations when this exercise can be helpful.

_____

_____
_____
_____
_____
_____
_____
_____
_____
_____
_____
_____
_____
_____
_____
_____
_____
_____
_____
_____
_____
_____
_____

Gratitude

Gratitude is more than just saying "thank you." It's a powerful psychological and emotional tool that can enhance our well-being, boost our mental health, and strengthen our relationships.

Gratitude is deeply rooted in psychology, and its effects on our minds and emotions have been extensively studied.

First of all, gratitude is strongly associated with positive emotions such as happiness, joy, and contentment. When we express gratitude, our brain releases dopamine and serotonin, the "feel-good" neurotransmitters.

In the long run, regularly practicing gratitude has also been linked to reduced symptoms of depression and anxiety. It helps shift our focus away from negative thoughts and promotes a more optimistic mindset.

Gratitude is a powerful social glue. When we express gratitude, it strengthens our relationships by conveying appreciation and fostering trust and reciprocity. Furthermore, we increase our self-esteem by recognizing and focusing on the positive aspects of our life and the accomplishments we have.

Gratitude should be a daily activity. Even though most people wait for a meaningful event in order to feel grateful, our everyday lives give us numerous situations to be grateful for. If we're not looking for something big, that is. Practicing and developing a habit of gratitude on a daily basis can help us improve our life and mindset just by making us look at the good side of life.

Gratitude
Journaling

Reflect on your life for a while. Recall some hardships that you went through and some accomplishments. Then, write a "thank you" letter to yourself, where you talk about everything that you've endured, learned, accomplished, etc. Express self-gratitude.

_____

*Note: Come back to this letter and re-read it whenever you feel anxious, sad, or have low self-esteem.

Gratitude
Exercise

This exercise aims to help you get in touch with your gratitude and be more aware of your mental representation of gratitude.

- Choose a comfortable and quiet space where you can reflect without distractions.

- Begin by taking a few deep breaths to relax your body and mind, focusing on your breath to center yourself.

- Then, try to bring yourself into a state of gratitude. To do this, answer these questions:
- Where in your body is gratitude placed? - Mentally stay in touch with that body part for a while.
- If gratitude would have a form, what form or shape would it have?
- What color would gratitude have?
- What material?

- Stay mentally in touch with the visualization of gratitude you made.
- How do you feel?
- What do you think?

- When you feel ready, open your eyes. Use the empty space below to paint a picture of your mental representation of gratitude.
- What does this representation mean to you?

Gratitude

Here is an exercise that can help you come up with all the things you are grateful for.

I'm grateful to nature for

_____

_____

I'm grateful to the world for

_____

_____

I'm grateful to God for

_____

_____

I'm grateful to the people around me for

_____

_____

I'm grateful to my parents for

_____

_____

I'm grateful to my friends for

_____

_____

I'm grateful to my partner for

_____

_____

I'm grateful to my children for

_____

_____

I'm grateful to my pets for

_____

_____

Gratitude
Journaling

Reflect on the things you wrote during the previous exercise. How can you show gratitude to the people around you? How can you incorporate gratitude into your everyday life and turn it into a habit?
To start the practice, at the end of your journaling, write 5 things you are grateful for from today.

_____

_____
_____
_____
_____
_____
_____
_____
_____
_____
_____
_____
_____
_____
_____
_____
_____
_____
_____
_____

Love

Beyond its romantic allure, love plays a profound role in our psychological well-being and the fabric of human society. Regardless of whether romantic, platonic, familial, or friendly, love is what connects us to other people and motivates us to care for them.

Psychologists and neuroscientists have recognized love as a basic human need. We are hardwired to seek and form social bonds from infancy, satisfying our needs for belonging and connection.

We feel love for our family, relatives, partners, friends, acquaintances, and pets. The love we feel makes us care for them and their needs, show appreciation and understanding, and provide help and assistance.

Love is a powerful force in promoting emotional well-being. Being loved and loving others enhances our mood, reduces stress, and increases feelings of happiness and contentment. Love fosters a sense of security and emotional resilience, helping us cope with life's challenges.

The other aspect of love is the love we feel from others. In early childhood, secure attachments formed through love and nurturing play a critical role in emotional and psychological development. They serve as a foundation for healthy relationships and emotional regulation later in life. Love in the form of attentive parenting provides a sense of safety and trust necessary for a child's healthy growth.

When we feel loved and appreciated, we gain self-confidence and self-esteem. Furthermore, we feel motivated and supported to accomplish our wishes and goals. Last but not least, we feel like we can lean on others for help, advice, guidance, and simple understanding and support.

Love
Journaling

Write a letter to your past self. Depending on the age you choose (you can also choose more "past selves" at different ages,) write what you love about yourself and what you appreciate and admire yourself for. Also, make sure that you provide loving guidance, advice or simply reassuring words to that past self.

_____

_____
_____
_____
_____
_____
_____
_____
_____
_____
_____
_____
_____
_____
_____
_____
_____
_____
_____
_____
_____

Love
Exercise

This exercise can help you get in touch with your representation of love and the sensations you feel when you think about love.

- Choose a comfortable and quiet space where you can reflect without distractions.

- Begin by taking a few deep breaths to relax your body and mind, focusing on your breath to center yourself.

- Then, try to bring yourself into a state of love. To do this, answer these questions:
- Where in your body is love placed? - Mentally stay in touch with that body part for a while.
- *Note: If you can't locate a body part on your own, focus on the area of the chest and the heart.
- If love would have a form, what form or shape would it have?
- What color would love have?
- What material?

- Stay mentally in touch with the visualization of love you made.
- What do you think?
- What associations come to mind?

- When you feel ready, open your eyes. Use the empty space below to paint a picture of your mental representation of love.

Love
Journaling

Reflect for a while on your relationship with love. How do you express love in your life? In what situations do you express love?

How do others express love toward you? Do you freely ask for love, attention, and affection, or do you passively wait for others to show you love? What belief guides that behavior?

_____

_____

_____

_____

_____

_____

_____

_____

_____

_____

_____

_____

_____

_____

_____

_____

_____

_____

_____

_____

_____

_____

Trust

Trust is a foundational element of human relationships and society itself. It is the unspoken agreement that underlies every interaction, from personal bonds to global partnerships.

Trust is the fundamental emotion that allows us to be spontaneous, honest, and free in front of the people around us. It's also an emotion with which we feel secure and protected, able to move forward through life and feel like there are people and things around us that can support and help us.

Trust, at its base, is an emotion that allows us to be vulnerable and open in front of people we trust, knowing that they will support us and won't abuse our honesty and openness. It is the belief that we can rely on others and that they will act in ways that consider our well-being. This belief creates a sense of security and emotional safety, crucial for healthy development. This vulnerability is essential for authentic connections and meaningful relationships.

Trust is a powerful stress reducer. In trusting relationships, individuals have a support system to lean on during difficult times.

Trust is also crucial for personal growth. It encourages us to take risks and explore new opportunities. When we trust ourselves and others, we are more likely to step outside our comfort zones, embrace change, and learn from our experiences.

Trust influences ethical behavior. When people believe they are trusted, they are more likely to act in trustworthy ways. This virtuous cycle promotes honesty, integrity, and moral behavior.

In conclusion, trust is not just a concept but a fundamental aspect of our psychology and social engagements. It shapes our relationships, influences our choices, and contributes to our emotional and psychological well-being.

Trust

The aim of these questions is to help you better understand your relationship with trust and where it stems from.

People I trust	People that trust me

Beliefs that allow me trust others are
_____
_____
_____
_____
_____

Beliefs that make me trustworthy are
_____
_____
_____
_____
_____

I communicate my trust in the following ways:
_____
_____
_____
_____
_____

Trust
Journaling

Reflect for a while on your relationship with trust. Do you tend to trust people easily, or are you more reserved and skeptical? What, for you, is a clear sign that you can trust someone? How long would you need in order to start trusting someone new? How do you react when someone disappoints you, and you lose your trust in them?

Inspiration

Inspiration is a wellspring of creativity, motivation, and personal growth.

Feeling inspired is the requisite for being creative, spontaneous, and adjustable to external circumstances that you can't control.

Inspiration is not just for artists and creative people to come up with ideas about art. It stretches far beyond just painting or writing music and includes all our inner wishes and impulses to do something new, come up with solutions to problems, or spend our free time.

Inspiration, at its base, is an emotion in which we feel motivated to do, create, or work through something and come up with solutions or courses of action.

Inspiration

These questions aim to help you identify the things and people you are inspired by.

Activities that inspire me	World events that inspire me

People around me that inspire me

Imaginary characters that inspire me	Famous people that inspire me

Inspiration
Exercise

Now, once you've identified the things and people that inspire you, it's time to tackle the reasons behind that inspiration. These two exercise can help you do just that.

- Find a quiet and comfortable space where you can reflect without distractions.

- Take a few deep breaths to relax and center yourself.

- Reflect on the answers you gave on the previous page.

- Go over each item or person you named and identify what exactly inspires you from them. If possible, explain it with just one word. Write those words down.

- Next, take a look at all the words you wrote. Are there any repeating patterns? If yes, what are they?

- How can you, in your everyday life, be more in touch with these things or people and be inspired by them?

- Think back to moments in your life when you felt truly inspired. These could be times when you were motivated, creative, or deeply moved by something.

- Write down one such situation.

- Describe what inspired you, how it made you feel, and the impact it had on your actions and mindset.

Inspiration
Journaling

Reflect on your relationship with inspiration. How often do you feel inspired to try out new things, come up with creative solutions, or improve yourself and your life by looking up to a inspiring person? What life areas can you be more inspired in? What do you need in order to be inspired?

Creativity

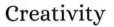

Creativity is a spark that ignites innovation, fosters problem-solving, and enriches our lives in countless ways. From the arts to science, business to personal growth, creativity is a force of transformation and a wellspring of human potential.

Creative thinking enables us to approach challenges from fresh angles. It encourages us to explore unconventional solutions and overcome obstacles with resourcefulness. Creativity is a valuable asset in both personal and professional problem-solving.

Creativity is also a powerful tool for personal growth and self-discovery. Engaging in creative actions, whether it's writing, painting, or crafting, allows individuals to explore their thoughts, emotions, and inner worlds. It nurtures self-expression, self-confidence, and a deeper connection with oneself.

Furthermore, creativity nurtures resilience by encouraging individuals to embrace change and uncertainty. It empowers them to adapt, navigate, and find new opportunities.

Creativity encourages us to see the world from different viewpoints. It challenges preconceptions, biases, and stereotypes, promoting open-mindedness and cultural awareness.

Engaging in creative activities, from cooking to gardening, brings joy and a sense of accomplishment. These activities are also linked to reduced stress levels and improved mental well-being.

Embracing and nurturing our own creativity can lead to a more vibrant, innovative, and fulfilling life.

Creativity

Content font and size

In my mind and belief system, creativity is
_____
_____
_____
_____

Do you consider yourself a creative person? Why?
_____
_____
_____
_____

Activities or hobbies make me feel most creative are
_____
_____
_____
_____

I am most creative when
_____
_____
_____
_____

The emotions that fuel my creativity are
_____
_____
_____
_____

Creativity
Journaling

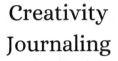

This journaling exercise is a Creative Flow Journaling. For the next couple of minutes, let your thoughts flow naturally and write everything down. Write down whatever pops into your head without censoring or editing. If you get stuck, simply write, "I don't know what to write," until your thoughts start flowing again.

Continue writing without stopping or pausing to read what you've written. After your chosen time period is up, take a moment to reflect on what you've written. Are there any insights, ideas, or themes that stand out to you?

_____

_____

_____

_____

_____

_____

_____

_____

_____

_____

_____

_____

_____

_____

_____

_____

_____

_____

Ending Words from a Therapist

I hope this letter finds you in a place of reflection and newfound self-awareness. Completing the shadow work workbook was an important step in your journey toward healing and self-discovery, and I want to commend you for your dedication and courage throughout this process.

Shadow work is not an easy path to walk. It requires a willingness to confront the hidden aspects of yourself, those parts you may have buried deep within. It's a journey into the depths of your own psyche, where you've encountered both light and darkness.

Shadow work is not about erasing or eliminating those darker aspects of yourself; it's about integration. It's about embracing your whole self, both the light and the shadow and finding harmony within. This integration allows you to live authentically without the weight of unacknowledged baggage holding you back.

Remember that healing is not a linear journey. There may be times when you feel you've made great strides and other times when you encounter setbacks. This is all part of the process.

As you move forward from completing this workbook, I encourage you to continue your self-care and self-reflection practices. Journal your thoughts and feelings, engage in mindfulness, and reach out for support when needed. You have the strength within you to face any challenges that arise.

Continue to lean on your support network as you move forward, and remember that your growth and healing are ongoing processes. Your commitment to your own well-being is a testament to your resilience and inner strength. With that, take the time to show yourself love, understanding, support, and gratitude.

Made in United States
Troutdale, OR
11/07/2023

14348764R00096